Urban Ministry

Revitalizing a Church and Impacting a Community

Rev. Dr. Jamesetta Ferguson,
D. Min., M. Div., M. Ed.

Edited by: Claude R. Royston

BK Royston Publishing, LLC
Jeffersonville, IN

BK Royston Publishing
P. O. Box 4321
Jeffersonville, IN 47131
502-802-5385
http://bkroystonpublishing.com
bkroystonpublishing@gmail.com

© Copyright – 2015

All Rights Reserved. No part of this book may be reproduced, stored in a retrieval system, or transmitted by any means without the written permission of the author.

Published by: BK Royston Publishing LLC
Cover design by: Jonathan Snorten
Layout: BK Royston Publishing LLC

ISBN-13: 978-0692325278
ISBN-10: 0692325271
LCCN: 2015940910

Printed in the United States of America

Dedication

I dedicate this book to my Lord and Savior Jesus Christ who gave me strength, wisdom and knowledge to write this book, my professors who walked me through the process, the St. Peter's United Church of Christ Louisville family, the entire Russell neighborhood and my entire family who support me in all that I do to provide Urban Ministry in love and excellence.

TABLE OF CONTENTS

Chapter		Page
	Dedication	
ONE	THE MINISTRY SITUATION	1
TWO	PRACTICAL THEOLOGY INTERPRETIVE BASIS FOR THE PROJECT	33
THREE	THE STRATEGY FOR THE STUDY	81
FOUR	INTEPRETING THE LEARNING OF THE PROJECT	113
FIVE	IMPLICATIONS OF LEARNING FOR FUTURE PRACTICE	139
	Appendix A	159
	Appendix B	161
	Appendix C	163
	Appendix D	171
	Appendix E	217
	ENDNOTES	219
	BIBLIOGRAPHY	228
	BIOGRAPHY	237

CHAPTER ONE

THE MINISTRY SITUATION

Introduction

Louisville is the largest city in Kentucky and many released from the Kentucky penal system seek refuge in Louisville believing their opportunities for better education, quality jobs and good housing are greater. St. Peter's United Church of Christ, a renewing church is located in the Russell neighborhood, which is an impoverished urban community already filled with hopelessness, scarcity and oppression. As part of this neighborhood, we as the St. Peter's faith community appear to see more than our share of those recently released from prisons and those other individuals or their family members that have a relationship with the local and state criminal justice system.

The church is situated within a one mile radius of the largest public housing partnership in Louisville, two correctional transitional housing facilities and one of the most successful addiction recovery facilities in the United States. Through participation in various ministries more than a few of the men and women released from these facilities expressed that they could not understand why they are unable to obtain and retain jobs even though they meet the basic job qualifications. Some mentioned becoming easily angered or having difficulty getting up to go to work because they lacked hope in long term employment or even had fear of performing the job adequately and consistently. The majority of these men and women shared that they were unable to maintain healthy and positive relationships with family members and friends because of past indiscretions, hurts and pain.

After meeting with them through the various church ministries, mission and other community events, the pastoral staff determined that even though they had completed their respective institutional programs, there appeared to be a lack of emphasis on emotional health and the building of positive relationships. Positive relationships are tools we believe necessary for the completion of the re-entry programs and successful utilization of a traditional skill set taught in most re-entry programs. Several effective re-entry programs throughout the nation suggest that successful ex-offenders must have a home that is safe, clean, sober and stable, along with access to guidance and support for addressing and adopting clean and sober lifestyles while attempting to transform their lives. The successful programs include guided program design that helps the individual change old patterns and make positive choices and decisions that are different from the path that got them involved in the criminal system, which for many began when they were children and youth. The Reverend Annie Rodriguez of Grace House in Chicago states, "The longer you're incarcerated, the less likely the person is able to make decisions for themselves."[1] As a result of making poor choices and decisions many of those released end up back in the penal system.

Consequently, we believe mentorship and positive life coaches will help the individual live a healthy and legally sound life. We at St. Peter's deem that a holistic approach which includes education and tutoring will help the ex-offender adopt a clean, working lifestyle which leads to a good job or creating a business that is legal, along with seeking out or re-entering into healthy and positive relationships with their neighbors and family members. Homer Ashby advocates that the black church enter into partnership with a variety of persons with different backgrounds and gifts so as to mobilize the most effective force against oppression, teaching them how to be family and community in those ways that have sustained and protected people in the past.[2] We at St. Peter's envision the church to be a shelter, a place of transformation, a place where individuals and families care for each other as they are nurtured through education, community service and healthy living, all of which is essential for a healthy community.

The purpose of this applied research project is to examine the effectiveness of a seven week program for ex-offenders transitioning back into mainstream society, utilizing a holistic approach to their re-entry programming which included not only traditional learning, but also life application of Christian principles, intentional nurturing, support and the accountability of the ex-offender to a supportive faith community and in turn the faith community's accountability to the ex-offender for establishing a mentoring relationship with them during their time of transition. We believe that the church and any

Christian based organization must have social gospel activism as part of the re-entry program and permanent behavior changes; otherwise we ignore the very principles of our Christian faith. It befits us individually and collectively as concerned people and as Christians to help prepare the marginalized, the oppressed, and the disconnected men and women in our society to become productive contributors.

This program will also address systemic forces which lead to incarceration, such as long-term spells of poverty and/or welfare dependency, individuals who lack training and skills and have either experienced periods of persistent unemployment, or have dropped out of the labor force altogether, and individuals who are frequently involved in street criminal activity.[3] The creation and partnering of multiple re-entry programs within our communities is essential to the continued decline in inmate recidivism.

The success of the program will be measured by the rate of recidivism of the participants in the program.

A Statement of the Situation and Need

The community in which we serve at St. Peter's is one of the poorest areas in Jefferson County. The population of this community is nearly 90% African descent. Located directly across the street from the church campus is the largest public housing complex in Louisville with 768 individual and family units. There is a high concentration of substance abuse rehabilitation facilities, such as the Healing Place and Volunteers of America, and safe places for homeless people, such as the Wayside Christian Mission. Also located within this urban society are the Dismas House and the Community Transitional Housing (CTS) for paroled and nonviolent offenders.

Dionne Jones, citing William Wilson in her book, *Teenage Pregnancy: Developing Strategies for Change in the Twenty-first Century*, notes that when you have these types of community demographics, it is described as having a critical mass, a self-sustaining chain reaction that creates an explosive increase in the amount of crime, addiction, and welfare dependency.[4] This critical mass is also perpetuated by the local school system that has a disproportionate amount of disciplinary patterns that systematically alienate or eliminate African American children from the school system[5], thus adding to an already uneducated or undereducated community.

The church also serves an area, where those living below the poverty level hovers around 44%.[6] Many residents are undereducated with less than high school diplomas, and a large proportion of those in the Russell community have a relationship with someone incarcerated and/or with persons having ties to the justice system. Because of the ethos of this community, in January 2012 when one thousand Kentucky inmates with Class D felonies were released in order to ease financial woes for the state it was estimated that approximately one third of these inmates came to Louisville[7], and are now living at the various agencies located within a mile of the church.

The current ministries at St. Peter's are designed to transform, empower and renew the lives of those we serve. As a church also in need of transformation and renewal, we became intentional in creating social ministries to address issues we saw within the neighborhood, such as addictions, scarcity in nutritional and healthy foods, and the lack of motivation and participation in educational opportunities.

Background of the Context and History

St. Peter's Evangelical Church, United Church of Christ, initially named The First German Evangelical Lutheran Church of the City of Louisville was organized on August 22, 1847 and has been located in its current location since 1849. This mainline German Evangelical and Reformed Church were made up of farmers, laborers, trade and craftsperson's located in west Louisville. As the members grew in their affluence, they became more privileged in their thoughts and behavior and concentrated on ministries inside the four walls of the church and not outside. Social mission was reserved for their members and German neighbors.

In the early 1950's-1960's, St. Peter's was highly successful in ministering to the needs of those they had identified as part of their community. However, as the composition of the neighborhood in which this church was located changed, the church did not effectively adapt to the changes surrounding them. As the neighborhood transformed to a predominately African-American culture, and because many of the members and their children had left the area or had found other churches to minister to their specific needs, the membership of the church began to decline. Because the church failed to adjust to the new culture, by 2006 the once vibrant membership of 1000 members was down to 34 of which only fifteen were active members. St. Peters had a succession of permanent and interim pastors at the church, but continued in a spiral of decline, I believe, because the model of ministry remained unchanged. Therefore in order to keep the doors of the church open, in December 2006, I was called to lead the church into a new direction and a ministry of revitalization.

In 2007, the church's vision changed and became to plant and cultivate seeds of necessity in our community through spiritual guidance and community partnerships, continuously seeking opportunities to educate, inform and empower the members of congregation and community to be effective advocates for themselves, families, friends and neighbors. A new mission statement more reflective of our social ministry and community was adopted; we are to be God's hands and feet at St. Peter's called to embrace and serve the marginalized and those persons who have been kicked to the curb, those ignored by society by being used as witnesses, and by proclaiming God's message, God's power, and God's salvation.

    The new St. Peter's United Church of Christ was intended to be a welcoming faith community. It was our goal to provide numerous benefits to the community including improved educational opportunities and a transformative justice model of ministry, focusing on communal transformation and change, rather than condemnation and judgment. This approach was designed not only as a feeling of hospitality, but was committed to being hospitable by being culturally sensitive to those we served based on historical, cultural, social, economic, and political forces that help shape urban America.

    The church began putting into practice what was fair and just by empowering those in our community to become effective advocates for themselves and their neighbors. While the majority of the people we minister to were African American, the ministry was envisioned to work toward the liberation of all who are oppressed and "kicked to the curb" by society. It was our goal to assist and advocate for persons and caregivers through the planning and delivery of services by a highly effective pastoral and lay staff in partnership with public and private organizations. Services were provided with respect, care and accountability for the good of the community. We became dedicated to helping people interpret the situation in which they live, and to recognize and identify specifically how they are treated in society. So to foster this social change information was gathered regarding the demographics of the community. Needs assessments were performed during church and outreach events and as a result of our findings various ministries were systematically established to address those identified needs. These needs were broken down into three ministry types: Ministries of Transformation, Ministries of Empowerment and Ministries of Renewal.

We will now explore the ministry types to contemplate if these new approaches to ministry would be effective in St. Peter's becoming a place where individual and family cares for each other as they are nurtured through education, community service and healthy living, all of which is essential for a healthy community.

Ministries of Transformation

In 2007, an addiction ministry was established by a new member of the church who was in recovery and had successfully transitioned from prison back into society. For over one year, the average attendance of the meeting was eight participants. But now, six years later the church currently hosts three Twelve Steps Alcoholics Anonymous (AA) meetings serving 750 men and women weekly, offering support and recovery from various substance addictions. Step One of AA encourages individuals to admit that they are powerless over alcohol and other substances and that their lives have become unmanageable. The Center for Disease Control (CDC) defines moderate levels of alcohol consumption for Americans as having up to 1 drink per day for women and up to 2 drinks per day for men.[8] Many of these men and women have admitted to consuming much more than the moderate amount daily for years, beginning as early as their preteen years, and finally admitting that their lives have become unmanageable. The risk factors for alcoholism and drug abuse which include frequency of use, age, sex, depression and other mental health problems, and social and cultural factors are explored within the program. We agree this program is empowering the individual to make a positive move toward sober, healthy living, but through internal review and discussions we also discovered it lacked the life application of Christian principles, intentional nurturing, support and accountability we believed is needed to sustain this transformed life.

Therefore, the areas that the church began to focus on were: depression and other mental health problems, and social and cultural factors. Through our work with current participants, we realized that addictive behaviors affected the individual's ability to complete education, hold-down jobs, and maintain healthy family systems, which many times are a result of poor mental health, and social and cultural stresses.

The second program of transformation established at the church was the establishment of a Dare to Care Food Bank onsite, addressing the cycle of hunger within the community. This weekly social ministry was started in July 2007 and today distributes 157,000 pounds food to over 13,000 people annually. Many nutritionists promote healthy eating as one of the best ways for the brain to develop, helping to fight off some mental health problems and chronic and infectious diseases. "Feeding America," a national food program states that insufficient nutrition contributes to the lack of children learning and adults from being able to maintain or be productive on jobs.[9] These vulnerabilities often lead to illegal addictive behaviors and criminal participation to combat these inadequacies.

The third social ministry of the church was formed out of an unsought opportunity. In 2009, we were approached by a retiree from the Kentucky Department of Corrections who had also served as warden of Luther Luckett Correctional Complex for several years. The purpose of the meeting was to allow residents within the community to share their concerns about allowing another halfway facility in the community for men being released from various Kentucky correctional facilities. The presentation revealed that many inmates being released ended up back in prison because of a lack of housing, job skills and adequate social support. It was explained to us that this facility would provide the necessary support and skills, in hopes that these men would successfully migrate back into society as productive citizens. Immediately upon the opening of the facility, 15-20 of the residents began to attend St. Peter's on a weekly basis for spiritual growth and direction. Through the process of extravagant welcome, the church leadership and members began to welcome the men from Community Transitional Services (CTS), not fully understanding the challenges these men faced and what these relationships would demand. The men were encouraged to take ownership in their lives and were encouraged and allowed to discuss their concerns and fears now that they were living on their own. Empowerment, the process by which an individual or group conveys to others the authority to act, was encouraged not only with these groups of men, but with all who came to the church no matter their life circumstances.

Ministries of Empowerment

The partnership with CTS was the beginning of the formation of the Ministries of Empowerment at the church. Several members of our faith community who were unemployed or underemployed were subsequently given opportunities for employment within the new CTS facility. This was a tremendous step for these newly hired individuals, which moved them toward individual empowerment; helping them to become active and productive citizens in the community.

Next the church ministerial staff embarked on individual learning through a revised program of Christian Education, relying on biblical stories and teachings, connected with life lessons to advocate overcoming oppression and injustice, through faith, endurance and perseverance. We established lessons for adults and youth to learn about the Christian faith and to make and nurture their commitment to live as followers of Christ. To build relationships between individuals and families, intergenerational activities with a spiritual education component were added to the curriculum. Empowerment was also fostered through Health and Wellness Programs, as individuals were encouraged to understand that part of good stewardship involves us realizing we are part of God's creation; therefore we are to become good stewards of our bodies.

Finally, compassion through volunteerism was promoted, and individuals were challenged and empowered to move beyond society's expectations for them and their families. We felt it important for those within this community to be allowed to move beyond their circumstances and to seek a "hand up" and not just a "hand out." This was done through compassionately helping others in times of need despite dealing with their own needs and struggles. The church now has an established program of volunteers of twenty to twenty-five individuals weekly serving in the various church missions.

Ministries of Renewal

Our participation in helping individuals and families also included advocating good quality and higher educational achievement levels for those living within the community. The education opportunities were being provided through educational resources located at and within the church, as well as partnering with other more experienced and designated education agencies throughout Louisville.

A Literacy Program was started in September 2007. Salary support from a local education institution for a program coordinator was obtained. This Literacy Program was intergenerational with meals so that learning and relationship building could take place in a healthy environment. Other educational partnerships within the Russell community were established to also help support this program.

An Outreach Coalition among other Russell neighborhood churches was established to promote Health Fairs and Community Forums with city and state representatives to discuss and address issues that directly affect residents in the community. Our goal was to go beyond individuals and families and to advocate changes in behaviors that caused some of the suffering that we saw from individuals coming through the church doors.

As part of ministries of renewal, there were programs established for restoring the family unit. Community workshops of advocacy and self-help partnering with local hospitals, health clinics and other grass root agencies to provide medical assistance and health education to the Russell community were held quarterly.

Finally, Christian fellowship and mission was nurtured through intentional and extravagant welcoming and affirming of all who entered into St. Peter's regardless of their journey in life. These were opportunities for ministry and openings to make a difference in helping transform men and women who are oppressed and down trodden. By being radically welcoming, a term used often by churches and members of the United Church of Christ, which is also a part of applying Christian principles, we chose to walk with these men and women in our community whether current residents or those reintegrating into society from the penal system. As a result of the various ministries and programs, we hope all regardless of their journey will be empowered to change their lives for the better.

Howard Thurman encourages us that as part of the human family, we must properly value ourselves in a way that transcends culture, context, and condition.[10] Through our ministries of empowerment we believed we were becoming an area community organization providing a vehicle to empower and promote proper value to individuals based on the understanding that we are all created in God's image and are all valuable in God's sight. Our ministries of transformation, empowerment and renewal were moving St. Peter's into becoming a 21st century mission within a Black Church context, the context in which the church was striving to make a difference.

Becoming a 21st Century Mission within a Black Church Context

The Black Church is considered the most important institution within the urban community, and because of its long history in dealing with social issues within the community, it must continue to have a voice for the oppressed and marginalized which it serves. In the United States, it is the black church that has defined social activity, proper behavior and appropriate living conditions for most African Americans. Professor Homer Ashby went on record as claiming the black church as the prime institution within the black community to carry African Americans forward into collective identify formation guaranteeing survival and fulfillment.[11] St. Peter's by virtue of being a part of the African American community functions culturally as a black church, though it, serves all races, ethnicities, gender and sexual orientations.

St. Peter's made an intentional choice not to assimilate the old and sometimes outdated ministry programs, worship ways or traditional practices of the original St. Peters Church and Mission. Becoming a 21st Century Mission within a Black Church Context meant reaching people where they are, realizing that many of the people we would serve today did not share a common culture, values or practices. We hoped to create a new sense of Christian identity within the community and because we were ministering to many of the unchurched, our programming had to include spiritual formation, helping those new in the faith understand and learn basic Christian beliefs and practices. Since part of our model is to help those in the neighborhood, we began living out the historical responsibility of the black church, which has always been the social agency that provided food and shelter in time of need, and has been the gathering place to address communal and racial issues.

As we serve in a black church context, we believe that the empowerment of and advocacy for individuals, the uniqueness of surrogacy inherent within the black church, and the gift of nurturing was a necessary component to the success of the mission. Both surrogacy and nurturing in the black church are not new concepts and have played major roles in the urban community for hundreds of years, including fostering hope to those persons without hope. The black church has served as family and the support system to those who are sometimes without relatives or friends due to various circumstances. The black church through history has been the institution within the community to develop and promote individual and collective education, family values and social change. The concept of surrogacy is a way of instilling self-worth and somebodyness[12] in people who otherwise have been invisible in society and deemed unworthy by those of privilege. Surrogacy in the black church has also been the voice for social justice and inclusiveness for those often ignored and relegated to second class citizenship by society.

    Surrogacy in the black church in the 21st century will continue to be a strong concept in the community as we deal with the realities of an environmental crisis, drug crisis, crisis in education, incarceration crisis, joblessness crisis, homelessness crisis, and unfortunately crises in love and the family. In this 21st century, we will become the institutional force that has lived out the Christian mission as taught from the time of slavery into this century.

It would be impossible to live out this vision of community transformation without St. Peter's addressing one of the basic and most prevalent ills of this community, and that is individually or family members that have a relationship with the local and state criminal justice system. It is impossible to ignore this component of "institutionalized slavery," a term defined as those forces that maintain second class citizenship through imposed oppression and other negative conditions against groups based on race and culture. Institutionalized slavery is undeniably present; keeping those marginalized obligated to a system of hand-outs and institutionalized dependency. One of the largest providers of institutional slavery is now the penal system. Michelle Alexander in her recent book

The New Jim Crow: Mass Incarceration in the Age of Colorblindness reminds us of tactics that have been used throughout each generation to support racial and class exclusion. These tactics include discrimination and exclusion seen through the form of taking away the basics rights of those who have had a brush with the criminal system.[13]

The need to deal with the realities of social failings and systems of inequality based on race and culture within our own community is essential. Kentucky's serious crime rate has been well below that of the nation and other southern states since the 1960s, and the current crime rate is about what it was in 1974. Nevertheless, the Commonwealth's incarceration rate went from well below to slightly above the national average between 1985 and 2009.[14] A preliminary inquiry reveals that several leading causes of Kentucky's prison growth include increased arrests and court cases, high percentage of offenders being sent to prison, technical parole violators and drug offenders. With respect to drug offenders, primarily cocaine possession, black offenders were incarcerated in 31.6% of cases, compared to 18.4% for non-black offenders. In the case of other misdemeanor crimes such as shoplifting, black offenders were incarcerated in 10.2% of cases, compared to 4.9% for non-black offenders.[15] In 2009 Kentucky also became known as having the 6th highest incarceration rates for females.[16] The commonality for both the male and female ex-offender is substance abuse, lack of education and poor work history

The challenge to deal with issues of oppression and injustice means that we as a church and mission must work to break the cycle of institutionalized slavery and that is done through our varied social ministries and mission. Individuals must be empowered to make the best life choices for themselves and their family, which is difficult in a prison culture where they have had to ask permission for just their daily existence. Freedom to choose (whether good or bad) and understanding the consequences of the choice on the community grants liberating power to the individual, we've learned, through life application of Christian principles, intentional nurturing, support and accountability of this faith community.

CHAPTER TWO

PRACTICAL THEOLOGY INTERPRETIVE BASIS FOR THE PROJECT

Becoming a Real-World Church and Mission in the United Church of Christ

The United Church of Christ (UCC) was formed on June 25, 1957 by the union of the Evangelical and Reformed Church and the General Council of the Congregational Christian Churches of the United States in order to express more fully the oneness in Christ of the churches composing it, to make more effective their common witness in Him, and to serve His kingdom in the world. The UCC is one of the more unique denominations because the church can trace its heritage to the Congregational and Christian Churches and the German Evangelical and Reformed Churches. This legacy has also caused some confusion and complication related to the inclusivity of church membership due to the merger of over 2 million members with different theology, polity and procedures into one denomination. However, this union was possible because all the traditions taught and agreed that Christ is the head of the church. Nevertheless, because of the ancestral beginnings of the various church traditions, the problem of identity has vexed the UCC as much and perhaps more than other denominations. The church has been influenced by a variety of theologies over the years. A document called "The Basis of the Union " outlined both the procedures to be followed in securing the union and principles on which the union would be based. [17] This document tells us that there are three participants in the Covenant and the first participant is God, and the other participants are the believer and his fellow believers. This covenantal relationship allows the movement of the Holy Spirit to work through us as believers being led by God, spreading the gospel of Jesus Christ to build the kingdom of God here on earth.

The church is composed of Local Churches, Associations, Conferences and the Synod and all work in a collaborative manner. The Constitution encourages us as the body of believers to respect, honor and support each other's work in the ministry and to seek God's will and be faithful to God's mission. In many respects, the UCC is Congregationalist, yet the basic unit of the life and organization of the UCC is the local church.[18] The Constitution of the UCC reminds us of our mutual Christian concern and dedication to Jesus Christ, that Christ is the Head of the Church, the one and the many share in common Christian experience and responsibility. It is professed that congregations of the UCC have inherent autonomy and are modifiable and that there is freedom and independence under the headship of Christ, but with this freedom are responsibilities and accountabilities of the local and national church for fellowship. The church is also called to live in a covenantal relationship with other congregations for the sharing of insights and for active cooperation among churches.

Despite all of the organizational, political and covenantal understanding, the real question then becomes how does all of this relate to God's people and how does it help to shape the ministries and missions of the Church? I suggest that as Christian believers, we are constituted by grace, and what holds the UCC together is a common faith in Jesus Christ and sets of covenant promises exchanged by the social existence and citizenship of the people within the church. The UCC is not a church that functions under coercion and control of church authorities. The church is a body of persons exercising freedom to listen, evaluate, decide and act through the discernment of the Holy Spirit.

This discernment means seeking advice, counsel, critique and support from those in the wider church, who are there to help in a collaborative manner. This suggests that members of the church are involved in ministries that they have been called into by God. This can be true on an individual basis, local, regional or a national scale. Members of the UCC are encouraged to minister to the people through the Word of God, but they should also be compassionate and passionate servants of Christ. The Church is called to love God's people and to effectively communicate with the members through listening, counseling and praying as tools to effective ministry. We are compelled to have spiritual discernment exercising character and integrity, trying to live according to the gospel. As denominational leaders in uniting the body of Christ in the way that our founding church leaders had envisioned, we are obligated to serve others proclaiming the gospel of Jesus Christ to all of God's people. We should be able to place the needs of others before our own, commit ourselves to doing concrete things to meet those needs and not looking for favors or restitution from the church we serve. This covenantal commitment is reflected in the liturgical life of the UCC, which promotes being responsive to God, bearing gratitude and confidence for all that God has done and is doing for the worshiper both directly and through the world, indirectly.

The symbol of the United Church is Christ is the Cross of Victory or the Cross Triumphant in recognition of Christ's death on the cross for our sins, and because of his death we now have victory over the death of sin. The emblem motto based on John 17:21 "That they may all be one," [19] reflects the inclusive nature the church promotes to all God's people, and is our charge as believers to fulfill the command of Jesus Christ as outlined in Matthew 28:19-20 which states, "Go therefore and make disciples of all nations, baptizing them in the name of the Father and of the Son and of the Holy Spirit, and teaching them to obey everything that I have commanded you."[20]

The UCC Statement of Faith is a declaration of gratitude to God. It is a testimony; it witnesses to the faith held by the church, and offers opportunity for all people of free mind to unite with the church, if they will, in praising God for his mighty works.[21] This statement also reminds us that as individual members, we are free to believe and act in accordance with our perception of God's will for our lives. We are called to live in a loving, covenantal relationship with one another, gathering in communities of faith, congregations of believers and local churches. That is who we are as members of the UCC and this is what the church forefathers envisioned the church to become from the very beginning of the Reformed movement.

How Being a Part of the United Church of Christ Informs this Project

A few years ago, the UCC coined a phrase as part of the UCC public branding, "Whoever you are, where ever you are on life's journey, you are welcome here!" The UCC has used this as an opportunity to welcome those who are normally rejected by society and the church. It is this branding that has publically presented St. Peter's, regardless of the social status of those walking through the church doors, as a welcoming church. This statement of acceptance has helped shape our ministries and missions with theology and actions that encompass the realities of the residents we serve and see in the Russell community. Opening the doors to all, meant that many who walked in for our various social ministries were familiar with law enforcement and the penal system either through personal or family experience. We began to discern that our church vision and mission, along with the church leadership had little experience with those who were products of the criminal justice system, and to be thrust into a ministry involving the justice system, was both frightening and rewarding. To welcome the stranger in a way beyond being lip service, even those with criminal backgrounds, with open arms proved more difficult than imagined because of embedded institutionalized behavior, which is not only limited to an orderly and dictated daily behavior, but includes a life filled with racism and to some extent a slavery mentality. The realities, we discovered, were that we were witnessing this institutionalized behavior in not only those transitioning from corrections, but with many of the people we serve. Neuger reminds us it is not until we step outside our own cultural privileged standpoint that we welcome diversity, nor can we minister fully to diverse perspectives and experiences beyond our own experiences. We began to step outside of our religiosity and study the dynamics of the community and partner with others organizations familiar with the justice system, including the national body of the United Church of Christ. The formation of this project was unfolding as we grew in our understanding of those affected by this social ill.

Program and Mission Development

In 2008, one in every 42 adults in the United States was either in prison, in jail, or on supervised release.[22] This number is worse for those of African-American descent, ranging from 42% to 85% depending on the communities within the United States.[23] Organizations like *Mission Behind Bars and Beyond*, a Louisville, Kentucky based Christian led re-entry and life skills program, formed to reconnect formerly incarcerated persons with positive community role models to assist in their transition from prison to community. This organization has been able to reduce recidivism and doing a tremendous work in our local community. We entered into a partnership with Mission Behind Bars and Beyond to discover new ways to address those who had been locked up and to walk with those leaving prisons. We initially mentored one newly released individual from Luther Luckett Correctional facility and within three months expanded our mentoring programs to small groups including residents of Community Transitional Housing. Our denominational background promoted cultural diversity, religious freedom, and justice for all despite challenges of social, economic and cultural tensions. As large groups of men and women were leaving the prison system and making their way back into conventional society, and St. Peter's, we realized that there were numerous social problems preventing us from helping these individuals integrate back into society. There was and still is a need to deal with the realities of social sin and systems of inequality based on race and culture, particularity people of African descent within our own community. Hans A. Baer tells us that much of the content of African American religion acts as a response to racism and social stratification in American society.[24] The prison system is the 21st century form of American slavery evident in disproportional incarceration rates between blacks and others in the United States due to racial and economic bias. There is a need for the church to make a greater effort to live out the true meaning of the church as a place where persons are judged not solely on humankind's or institutional justice but also upon God's redemptive and restorative justice. The creation and partnering of other re-entry programs within our faith communities will be instrumental to the continued decline in inmate recidivism and improved social health in our urban communities.

We also began to see these types of partnerships as opportunities to emphasize the responsibility of each of us to promote the values of positive relationships, as well as an opportunity to show Christ like concern for others as a model of healing and wholeness of the marginalized, the broken and excluded part of our society. As a place of welcome, the goal of this urban church is to provide meaningful, educational opportunities and instruction that meet individual needs. The whole community benefits by enhancing the individual person and highlighting areas of need. The benefits of being a part of the St. Peter's faith community are designed so that all people are an integral part of this neighborhood church and will benefit by working and living in agreement with the African Proverb, "It takes a village to raise a child."[25] This Nigerian Proverb emphasizes the value of family relationships, parental care, and self-sacrificing concern for others, sharing, and even hospitality. While this saying is normally applied to the rearing of children, I take this opportunity to broaden the meaning to emphasize the responsibility of each of us to promote the values of positive relationships. As participants of the "village" we are instructed to understand that what one member of a group does has ramifications on the entire village. Therefore, as a community, we are interconnected and must help one another in order to create positive outcomes. Unfortunately, being interconnected is something that we have lost in this society particularly in the African American community. Therefore, as a community and as part of the St. Peter's village, we teach that we are interconnected and must help one another in order to create and foster positive outcomes. Mother Teresa diagnosed social ills in this way, "we've just forgotten that we belong to each other."[26] Kinship is what happens when we realize this goal. Through kinship, other essential things fall into place; without it, there is no justice, no peace. I suspect that with kinship as our goal, we would no longer be promoting justice—we would be celebrating it. It is our hope that St. Peter's becomes a place of hope, justice, peace and kinship; a place where you are treated like you are coming home, no matter where you find yourself in life.

The UCC Wider Church Ministries and Its Missions

We as Christian believers and members of the UCC churches are accountable for our actions to Christ first, as our sole head, then to each other in love. These beliefs are put into action through programs of the UCC Wider Church Ministries and its missions. The main mission of the Wider Church is to encourage and support members of the UCC to participate in the global, multiracial, multicultural, ecumenical and interfaith- missions by promoting accessibility to all.[27]

One such program is the United Church of Christ Justice and Witness Ministry (JWM), a ministry established to help build a stronger faith-based movement for peace, justice, equality and inclusivity. The historic commitment of the United Church of Christ to strive for justice and compassion is underscored through the work of Congregationalists, who over two centuries ago worked to free the African captives who were illegally brought to America on the ship La Amistad.[28] Congregationalists fought and struggled over the vision of love, justice and human freedom in God's world for 53 black Africans in 1839, and the ministry of the JWM in the twenty-first century is struggling for the same by showing compassion for those that are oppressed and marginalized, and those that are demoralized and exploited. JWM promotes justice in public policy channeling hope and imagination into power for good.[29] Therefore, JWM and the UCC as a whole, fight for issues such as criminal justice, human trafficking, women and children justice, gun violence and Lesbian, Gay, Bisexual and Transgender (LGBT) justice. In addition, they fight for issues such as racial and economic justice. Our task as the church is to respond through the presence of social action and concern for justice by showing love and unconditional acceptance of all people. We further respond to the needs of people who are suffering, whether physical or spiritual, believing that acceptance is what will unify us as the body of Christ.

Another program of the Wider Church Ministries is the UCC Health Care Justice Ministries (HCM) which recognizes worldwide health concerns and the work of health and human service. In 1991, the leadership of the UCC challenged the Church to renew and strengthen its commitment and involvement in advocating for health care for all as one way to respond to the priority Jesus gave to ministering to those who are sick based on the biblical text Matthew 25:31-46.[30] Today this ministry operates with the premise that healthcare is a basic right for all people and that the church has a moral responsibility to ensure that all of God's people, including the least of these should have access. The HCM promotes that a caring society does not condemn those to a life of chronic illness, lack of health care, abuse, neglect, and possibly death. As part of the body of Christ with many parts, Minister Barbara Baylor reminds us that "We need each other. If one is ill then all of us are not well! What happens to one happens to all!"[31]

    The United Church of Christ is dedicated to meeting human need without asking further questions, simply because it is human need. As a believer and a participant in the covenant, mercy and justice for all of God's people is essential. Just as Jesus helped those in need, regardless of social status, we must take on the attitude of Christ and support and love each person created in God's own image. Author George McKinney discusses holiness as described by Reinhold Niebuhr as an act of sanctification translated and interpreted by Jesus through inclusive love.[32]   His love for all of God's people was revealed through his acts of compassion for those that were oppressed, demoralized and exploited.

This project is intended to provide opportunities for effective life changing ministry and open doors that will make a difference in helping transform men and women who are oppressed and down trodden, including those coming out of the prison system. In a radically welcoming manner, which is a part of applying Christian principles, we have intentionally chosen to walk with these men and women as they reintegrate into families, neighborhoods and society in general. As a result, we hope they will be empowered to change their lives for the better. As an integral part of society, including these men and women, we must reflect our biblical teachings by remembering that we are not islands unto ourselves and that we need one another as part of the human family. Therefore, the church must become the catalyst for change and transformation as part of our moral compass. This process of transformation must include empowerment or self-determination and pride in who we are despite our circumstances. In order to empower these individuals, it is important to treat the entire self, mind, body and soul to attain wholeness.

St. Peters UCC recognizes that as a community organization we must provide a vehicle to empower and promote proper values to individuals based on their understanding that we are all created in God's image and are all valuable in God's sight. This transformation of proper values begins through acts of justice, equality and inclusivity, as well as health care, which promotes a holistic approach to healing; treating the entire self, including physical, mental, social and spiritual health.

Summary of Literature from Human Sciences and Reflection on How It Informs this Project

Through Jesus Christ as our example and the following theologies as models of God at work in the world, those who are oppressed are transcended beyond social and economic boundaries through the acceptance, compassion and love of all people, particularly those who are rejected by society and unfortunately to some extent the church. As Jesus participated in acknowledging the suffering of the poor, he proclaimed to them the good news of justice and freedom. The church and its organizations, must engage in the struggles of all humankind regardless of race, ethnicity, gender or economic status, including those who have had a brush with the law. Jesus offered sacrificial love to the outcast through his death and work of redemption, so who are we to do otherwise? This ministry is situated in the heart of a community that is poor and oppressed, so theologies that address the relevancy of the situations in these communities were chosen to provide the theological framework. Practical theologies that address the lives and conditions of the people that flow through the ministries and missions at St. Peter's UCC were chosen. Liberation theology was chosen because it speaks to helping people to become physically and spiritually free from the social issues that hurt and bind them to a life of suffering. A black theological framework was selected because it reflects the current make-up of this faith community; while we are a part of a mainline European American denomination we function in a predominately African American community with an African American pastor, facing issues of segregation, racism and classism in our daily lives. Finally, feminist and womanist theological frameworks were selected because they offer the practice of nurturing and surrogacy for those to whom we minister in this community, individuals many times suffering from fractured and broken family relationships.

Liberation Theologies

Theologian and civil rights activist, Martin L. King, Jr., wrote that people everywhere have the right to have three meals a day for their bodies, education and culture for their minds, and dignity, equality and freedom for their spirits.[33] This personal and liberal theology caused him to sacrifice himself not just for his human rights, but for the rights of all human kind. Through his transformation as a theologian and his formation as a Baptist religious preacher and leader, he picked up the mantle of the social gospel, not because it was self-serving, but because he believed that love is the only force that can change enemies into friends, and that unconditional love brings hope and reconciliation to those who are hurting from the ills of society.

Unconditional love motivates us to empower those that are poor, despised, oppressed and afflicted so that we all may know God's justice and peace. Unconditional or absolute love is defined by our church vision as wanting the best for all people and encourages those in the faith to give their lives for others, even as Christ did for us. When Dr. King spoke of a dream that would include justice for all, he spoke of a time when the community would be unified with open hearts for the common good of all of God's children, a vision where we would trust the Spirit of God to guide and move us toward a society of equality and love for one another. What better place to model this than in the church, a place where the spirit of unity should not be bound by race, class, gender, or privilege, but exists "wherever the heart is kind and collective will and the private endeavor seek to make justice where injustice abounds."[34] Heaven here on earth would be to live together in a community where there is not so much depression and hatred all around, but a community filled with hope, dignity and appreciation for self and the lives of others.

    Dr. King, as he was going through a transition in the ministry initially found himself attracted to liberal theology.[35] But as the transition evolved he began to question why the church was not more responsive to the social ills of society. He began to speak of a social gospel that deals with social reform as taught by Jesus. I too have an abiding faith in a God who has both a comforting personal presence and powerful spiritual force for decency and justice for all.[36] I believe the church must become a catalyst for social reform. Consequently, it is envisioned that St. Peter's United Church of Christ live out a social gospel where the words of segregation, racism, poverty do not exist and where the violent acts of a young man murdered, a woman beat up, a friend on the street from drug use or alcohol addiction, idle hands and crime make people feel uncomfortable enough to want to reject it, and do something positive and life changing to improve their individual situation and the community in which they live. Poverty has a devastating impact on the family life system, which is many times revealed through poor multi-problem families, female-headed households, little extended family ties, and reliance on government and private agencies to help meet daily and predictable life events.

    The church model for this urban community is to flourish in the righteousness of God. We must "See that justice is done, let mercy be our first concern, and humbly obey our God."[37] To do justice, we must love what is right, not what is wrong! Kindness means that we joyfully and cheerfully use our diversity and uniqueness in this faith community to make a positive difference in our community. Finally, we must make it our regular duty and business to please God first and that is reflected in how we treat one another, understand the truth of human life and God's destiny and purpose for our lives.[38] What a wonderful dream God's kingdom here on earth, but now let us deal with the reality of living in an American urban community in 21st century and in our context of a predominantly African American community and church.

Black Theologies

The National Committee of Black Churchmen wrote over two decades ago, that for black people "freedom was the gospel" and that when preached it causes us to forget momentarily about our despair and powerlessness and brings hope of a liberating Jesus that will set the captives free from the forces of social, political and economic oppression.[39] There are many systemic and institutional issues that must be dealt with and not ignored just because we are part of the United Church of Christ or any other mainline denomination. Policies and doctrines are in place, but the racial divide and the air of privilege remains the elephant in the room and this can only be improved through sacred and difficult conversations about the realities in which African Americans and other disadvantaged and oppressed people experience in this modern day America.

    Howard Thurman, Black Theologian and author of the book "Jesus and the Disinherited", believes that fear, helplessness and anxiety about our existence in society helps foster oppression, complacency and injustice. Dr. Thurman suggests that the under privileged and down cast of society are motivated by various forms of fear that are a result of helplessness about their situation, and that the outcast have anxiety about their existence in society. He further proclaims that it is blasphemous to care for people's souls while ignoring their need for food, shelter and human dignity and that all of these social ills can be addressed through love, just as Jesus offers us all unconditional love.

This implies that as Jesus participated in the suffering of the poor, and proclaimed to them the good news of justice and freedom, so must our church engage in the struggles of all humankind regardless of their oppression. Thurman states that, "Christianity as it was born in the mind of this Jewish teacher and thinker appears as a technique of survival for the oppressed".[40] Jesus offered sacrificial love to the outcast through his death and work of redemption, and he himself was living in a climate of deep insecurity. Therefore, Jesus faced a narrow margin of civil guarantees that he had to find some other basis upon which to establish a sense of well-being. Deep from within that order he projected a dream, the logic of which would give to all refuge. Through Jesus Christ as our example, that security is transcended beyond social and economic boundaries through the acceptance, compassion and love of all people, particularly those who are rejected by society and even those thrown away by the church.

Biblical teachings tell us that the church is called to be a place of worship and social action that is not bound by race and ethnicity, and is also a public institution that intentionally reaches out to various races and ethnic groups in any community. The United Church of Christ, with its largest church located in the urban community of Chicago, boasts of being liberal and being headed by an African American which has a tremendous history in advocating for justice and freedom around the world. However, that UCC ideology has been somewhat silent in Metro-Louisville/Jefferson County and continues to struggle nation-wide with inclusivity and splintering because the denomination has become too non-European American and demonized as being too liberal.

Over the past seven years the African American clergy in the urban Metro Louisville community have been paying close attention to our individual understanding of our role as the church in the urban community. We are from various Christian dominations ranging from Baptist, Pentecostal, Christian Methodist Episcopal, African Methodist Episcopal, Presbyterian, and United Church of Christ; and are a good representation of the African American Church. While we differ in life experiences, doctrine and culture, we all have been conditioned to believe that the Christ we serve and the doctrines that we follow were formed with all of God's people in mind. Often I have been accused of being too militant and black, but for me the relevant truth is there are systems and ideologies in place that uphold particular systems within society that hold down African Americans, as well as other oppressed and marginalized people. The God that most of us were raised to believe is white in ideology and supports and favors those people in society with power and privilege. This truth is reflected in the social sins of society that the majority of African-Americans and those oppressed must endure on a day to day basis. It is also reflected in many self-destructive behaviors that land many poor people and people of color in the penal system. Thomas Hoyt, Jr. tells us that there is something profound about the truth, for in the final analysis it relates to everything significant in our lives.[41] Our truth begins by teaching both black and white communities about the injustices that are unique to the urban and black cultures and their respective life experiences. Only then can the African American church start to address injustice and inequality issues. Without dealing with these truths our good works as Christians become short sighted and temporary. James Cone and Gayraud Wilmore tell us, especially for Black Christians that we must not be forced to choose between assimilation into a conventional form of White Christianity, and commitment to their own sense of religious particularity and chosenness, but that we must be able to be and express Christianity in ways that reflect who we are and realities in which we exist[42]

At St. Peter's we communicate to our faith community, a form of black theology that is liberating but also a survival theology.[43] We adamantly proclaim, no matter who we are, that we must have faith in a God who promised through the divine Word of God that one day we would all be free from oppression. We refuse and resent being held captive to the identification of being under classed and as James Cone would say, "The unwanted" of society. We preach and teach theology that encourages everyone to examine themselves individually and collectively to see how we can deal with the subjective grounds of reality.[44] We promote and have dialogue regarding creating heaven for our lives here on earth and not waiting until we get to heaven. We proclaim a sense of hope based on the perspective of our faith in Jesus Christ, not based on color or culture, but based on who brings us individual salvation through his death and crucifixion; thus, making this action of redemption an instrument for survival.[45] Instead, we declare that God is love and that God birthed the divine Jesus that fought the complacency of the marginalized people and those people in power, believing that a Jesus fought to save the masses, not just individuals. We have a unique opportunity in our churches to teach and preach about a Jesus who was compassionate, but was also an advocate for those that are powerless. This is reinforced by challenging the local and wider church to truthfully deal with the issues of injustice and oppression such as sickness, hunger, death, family, housing, crime and education. Jesus is real and life changing and the church and the biblical teachings and life application as the backdrop can make a difference in the lives of the people that it affects.

The church, in particular, the black church must play a crucial role in dealing with these realities of injustice in urban America which many times lead to incarceration. James O. Stallings suggests that in "the African American church, evangelism historically meant "freeing black folks" souls from sin and their bodies from physical, political, and social oppression, of setting the conditions of existence so that they could achieve full humanity."[46] Stallings also proposes that one of the most effective ways of dealing with injustices that African Americans experience is by conveying these wrongs in society through the vehicle of storytelling in the church.

Noted author Rev. Dr. Stephen Ray tells us that social sin is a reality that must be taken seriously and about which Christians must speak.[47] We must not just speak words, but God's truth. Despite the pushback by some within our area churches, it is crucial for the local church to reflect and speak the truth on matters of unfairness and injustice. We must boldly lead by example and model behavior, procedures and structures of justice and love of God to all, including for those returning to our community from a stay in prison. These truths no matter how difficult and heart wrenching can become tools of empowerment and hope when told as part of biblical witnessing, stories of faith and life experiences that speak of victories against all odds, given through the divine presence of God. Stories of our faith in God are not a new revelation, but consist of spiritual values that have been a part of the lives of African Americans from Africa to slavery to today. African culture was steeped in human relations, humanity's individual and corporate relationships to the supernatural and understanding of self and purpose. For many men and women forced into slavery, their faith was reoriented to deal with the atrocities that they were living and experiencing each and every day. Therefore, their understanding of God and their need to make sense of their situation became a part of their Christian understanding and daily practices. Edward Wimberly suggests that "biblical stories are a major resource for the listening and revising process because of the historic influence of the black Christian churches."[48]

The stories of God and the Bible were often told in relational stories in a format that came from the African Oral Tradition of storytelling. Reading was forbidden in most slave sites, so the preacher often dramatized the biblical stories to connect the bible to the slaves living conditions. While this was a way of building faith among the listeners, it was also a tool of survival from the slave masters listening for signs of rebellion. In Chapter 4 of Cone's book *God and Black Suffering: Calling the Oppressors to Account*,[49] he notes that black slaves were struggling with their understanding of who Jesus was, and how Jesus could allow the oppression, hardship and bondage they were experiencing as slaves. The slaves questioned if God was a liberator of the oppressed, then why were they suffering under the evil of slavery. God had delivered Moses from Pharaoh's army, Daniel from the Lions' Den and the Hebrew children. The slaves pondered why they were still in wretched conditions believing that God could end this evil condition with one righteous stroke. These are difficult questions that are still relevant today!

Many people still wonder whether God is just and right, refusing to believe that the sadness and pain of the world can cause them to lose faith in the power of God. Many have withstood pain and sufferings that are beyond mental comprehension. Yet, they remain resistant because of their faith. The oral tradition stories that they hear week after week foster a different type of survival for those in bondage. Reinhardt Niebuhr advances the thought that justice begins, not with theory, but with the concrete realities of injustice experienced by the oppressed and illumined by the God of the Bible. [50] The stories of the bible are the stories of our faith. These stories illuminate our understanding of our freedom struggle, in biblical and contextual form through our biblical foundation. The Word of God and the oral stories are intertwined to help people make sense of their oppressive environment. Their hope of freedom and justice are increased as they project their situation into the liberating stories in the Bible. It is taken for granted that God is righteous and will vindicate the poor and the weak. God liberated those in bondage in the bible, freed our ancestors and will continue to set the captives free.

Feminist and Womanist Theologies

St. Peter's has become a church that promotes survival and wholeness for the entire Russell community.[51] This wholeness is fostered through using maternal characteristics normally attributed to women and mothers. It was somewhat uncomfortable naming and claiming the use of these feminine gifts in the ministry, for fear that it would hamper my leadership as a woman senior pastor in the church and this community. As a product of the feminist movement living in a gender oriented society, to embrace these motherly instincts would somehow make me appear weak and less capable. However, applying these attributes to the ministry supported the ministry and mission at St. Peter's in ways never dreamed possible. It has been liberating for many and has brought healing to many men and women in pain.

While the United Church of Christ has been affirming to my call as a pastor of a church, women have historically, in the African American Church been oppressed and suppressed in using these gifts in a structured ministry for all people, whether male or female. Women have traditionally been the majority in black churches, yet their roles have been in most cases subservient or have served as quasi leaders behind the scenes. It has been difficult and humbling to use these maternal attributes, yet these qualities have been perceived as liberating and spiritual gifts to help this urban community become whole. Karen Baker-Fletcher tells us that "when people bring God with them to church, it is possible to find God in church if one is able to love the people as well as God."[52] Our acts of love used in the ministry and missions at St. Peter's offers liberation, hope and transformation to fractured lives using feminine strengths that we have often encountered in biblical text. We offer hope as women and leaders modeling behaviors of strength, character and fortitude despite the difficult challenges we face in doing ministry in caring ways that speak comfort and empowerment to those in our charge. Townes reminds us just how powerful hope really is, "It enables us to press onward when we feel like giving up. It enables us to draw strength from the future to live in a discouraging present. It makes it possible for us to see the world not only as it is, but also as it can be. Hope can move us to new places and turn us into new persons."[53] We offer optimism to those in our community who are hopeless about their current situations and sometimes bleak future.

Transformation of any disenfranchised community must also contain the gift of nurturing; a means of nourishing and cultivating those within the community. Recently, I attended a pastoral workshop with over seventy of my pastoral colleagues. During dinner one evening it was mentioned that many within the faith community, including those transitioning from prison, come to our faith community because of the nurturing feelings that they experience during times of worship, learning and fellowship. One of the white female clergy seemed appalled at our nurturing techniques and adamantly announced, "I'm not going to be anybody's mother or parent. They all have parents and that's not my role." This type of response clearly shows a lack of understanding as to the nurturing experience in the black church and part of our role in the urban community. The church or its representatives must become the welcoming place where people who are not grounded in nurturing and liberating relationships can come for this type of grounding. The church may be better served by remembering that God and his son Jesus were all about nurturing and cultivating relationships spiritually and humanly. Nurturing is not intended to parent individuals and take away their right of choice, but is a way to walk with the individuals and affirm and empathize with their journey of life; agreeing that we all live with trials and tribulations, but there is victory through Christ Jesus.

Edward Wimberly summarizes the role of the pastor in the nurturing process as one who creates an environment of concern and care, enabling worshipers to sing and pray, keeping the needs of people and the community in mind, and using Scripture and proclamation in ways that contribute to the ability of those in crisis to have courage and strength sufficient to move through emotional and interpersonal challenges. Nurturing must also be approached in a holistic fashion, addressing the all-around needs of the individuals and family unit. The holistic functioning of nurturing include: (1) Healing which pertains to binding up wounds or restoring bodily wholeness and mental functioning caused by disease, impairment, or loss, (2) Sustaining which consists of the provision of comfort and strength needed by people to endure difficult circumstances, (3) Guiding which refers to helping people through the provision of principles or educing within people choices, courses of actions, and resources in times of trouble, and (4) Reconciling which seeks to reestablish broken relationships or to bring people in positive relationship with others and God. The realities of our communities and the context in which we minister teach us that there is an overbearing need for nurturing and encouragement by the church for all people faced with marginalization, oppression, and a widening range of concerns.[54]

Finally, Womanist and Black Liberation Theologians Katie Cannon and Peter Paris introduce the concept of the Black Church as a surrogate world, a place that encourages human flourishing in the midst of seemingly insurmountable odds. The black church is a place where faith and hope are offered in ways to transform the circumstances of our lives into a lived reality of what the world should be like if all things were equal. This surrogate place also inspires self-esteem and worth to all individuals instilling in them a sense of 'somebodyness'[55] through positive leadership, Christian teachings and nurturing. Not only are spiritual values encouraged and embodied, physical needs are also addressed and met, with the understanding that as our relationship with God develops and matures, we begin to recognize the value of true relationships with one another, even those who are unlike us, wanting everyone to experience God's best and wholeness.

Becoming a Real-world United Church of Christ Church and Mission has brought about transformation not only in the individuals that we serve at St. Peter's, but also in the ministries and missions of St. Peter's. We have discovered that God's power of change is interweaved in all of creation and when we recognize the need for positive change, whether individually or as an institution, the possibility of wholeness is attainable.

CHAPTER THREE

THE STRATEGY FOR THE STUDY

Goals of the Learning Project

The goals of the learning project were developed with an emphasis on providing spiritual direction for the men reentering normal society, and determining their understanding of certain individual life skills based on their theological framework prior to participation in the life skills program and then at the conclusion of the program. Men coming from Community Transitional Service were engaged in sacred conversations during pastoral care sessions. It was determined that their experiences with reentry programs tended to address the traditional skill set which includes basic education, housing, employment, and sobriety through working the substance abuse twelve steps program. However, there appeared to be a lack of emphasis on emotional health and the building of positive relationships, tools necessary for the completion of the reentry programs and successful utilization of a traditional skill set. More than a few men expressed anxiety in gaining positive employment despite meeting basic qualifications. Others mentioned fear and lack of confidence in their abilities to sustain employment and positive family relationships. The majority expressed anxiety in having the freedom to make choices for themselves after being institutionalized, living for many years under the condition of being told their every move day in and day out. As we developed St. Peter's as a place of compassion and an educational resource, we began to look at the needs of the ex-offender from a pastoral care prospective, documenting, researching, and evaluating the poor self-esteem issues of the men and their fears and anxieties of being accepted in society. Robert Beckford, in his book "Dread and

Pentecost" describes the "Black Church as a shelter or rescue, a place of radical transformation, driven by the Spirit and a family".[56] We hoped that as we ministered to the men in various capacities that the overall church would be perceived as not only a shelter and place of transformation, but also a model of family that cares for each other as we are nurtured and taught through the support of the church and gain a deeper understanding of Christian beliefs and values. This project was developed directly from this supportive relationship, with an emphasis on providing spiritual direction for the men.

The project allowed for eight weeks of informative and small group discussions with minimally supervised ex-offenders. The concept was derived from a Doctor of Ministry Project taught at St. Peter's United Church of Christ in 2010 by CPE supervisor, Vickie Johnson. Dr. Johnson, a trained clinical psychologist, suggested that persons in the urban community, particularly African Americans are not encouraged to deal with their emotional health. It was her professional opinion that often people of color, because of their cultural upbringing, are discouraged from acknowledging emotional sickness and the need for professional support.[57] Her project focused on the training of clergy and lay leaders teaching them how to deal with various emotional health issues within their faith community. In the project, clergy and lay leaders served as gatekeepers for those congregants who might need additional support over and above pastoral care. Her program design allowed for 60-90 minute sessions offered during church school, bible study or informal worship services. The contents of the lessons included a handout titled "A War Between Flesh and Spirit: (1) Faith/Works, (2) Adolescence, (3) Transformation, (4) The Dark Night of the Soul and (5) Parenting. These handouts approached the emotions of fear, depression, rebellion, homosexuality, grief and boundaries as humanity's struggle with good and evil based on the biblical passage Romans 7:21. At the conclusion of the 30 minute oral presentation of the lesson, the groups no matter the size were encouraged to break off into smaller group discussions led by small group facilitators, with additional resources available for those who might self-identify that they need additional support.

As trained facilitators involved in the project, I found the handouts to be quite informative, and there was a great deal of positive response from those participating in the sessions. However, I was able to identify what I thought to be a few weaknesses within the design of the program. First, the lessons were offered once per month for eight months leaving little time for discussion and retention after the presentation of the material. There were huge gaps in follow-up for those identifying a need for emotional help. Second, the material was too clinically oriented and not written in lay language for easy understanding of the emotional issues. Third, the facility in which the lessons were taught was too large, sometimes in excess of 150 participants in the sanctuary, and the space was too restrictive for small group discussions. Fourth, the sessions did not allow for safe and confidential discussion of individual issues. Finally, for those who did identify an emotional need, often they were simply given reading material with no individual follow-up for additional support. As a result of our participation in the program, and by being a test site for the project, we recognized that if the lack of emotional health was prevalent in this non-restrictive community, then what were those reentering society from prison experiencing and how had their emotional health been ignored and neglected. Therefore, a new approach to address the emotional health issues was designed with the inmate/released persons in mind, with a desire to branch out at a later time to those within the St. Peter's faith community and the entire Russell community at large. Despite my personal concern with the format and the biblical hermeneutics of Romans 7:21 to characterize various behaviors and emotions, the sessions opened my eyes to the need for conversations and recognition by the church to address the mental and emotional health needs of the community.

St. Peter's Life Skills Coaching Program

The focus of the project was to observe the free-will choices of the participants of this program during program participation and after they are released from CTS. The participants were encouraged to make positive and healthy choices for themselves; along with maintaining a proactive approach to dealing with their emotional health, believing it will help them make the transition back into society more stable and manageable. A part of the practicum would determine if practical theology and spiritual formation using a biblical framework on life skills would have a positive effect on the participants while promoting personal and spiritual growth.

A small booklet format was developed as a guide for discussion, tailored with information to help address the anxieties expressed by the men during weekly Bible Study or pastoral care sessions. These anxieties were deemed widespread in the lives of these men expressing a desire to make positive changes, and as a result it fostered emotional instability and concern to them for the future.

The St. Peter's Life Skills Coaching Program was intended to enhance life skills and promote positive decision making skills for the men in various stages of the reentry program within CTS and was taught as part of the Men's Bible Study. These times of ministry have been a part of the church and CTS for the past two years and seem to allow the easiest access to participants. The program would also be available to other ex-offenders within the faith community that were referred to the pastor for support and pastoral care. The program was centered on how the Bible guides, directs, and instructs (empowers) individuals struggling with certain issues; communication; love; trust; expression; and accountability within the context in which they live.

The intent of each lesson is not to impose the literal translation of the scriptures on each participant, but to present biblical stories along with available clinical and social resources, in hopes that the participants will learn to make better emotional choices for their lives. The foundation of the program was to draw on the Christian upbringing of the participant, reflecting on how this framework may have an effect on their judgment, shaping how they dealt with the world around them and influence the choices that they make on a daily basis. The men identified struggles because of the lack of positive relationships with those with whom they interacted, whether family, friends, co-workers or the people around them, which were highlighted and discussed with their peers. Biblical examples of positive relationships for those living in healthy communities were explored. The lack of positive relationships, which often manifests as poor self-esteem and the effects on others, was addressed. Living in the community and functioning with others who are different in a respectful and caring way was discussed using scriptural references as keys to the discussions. Their interaction with one another during the classes was used as an example of how emotions can be masked in multiple layers of appearances causing both negative and positive responses. The layers of appearances to be addressed include grief, depression, anger and fear, and how the recognition and response to these emotions might directly shape their ability to retain jobs, live and work with others in a positive and healthy manner.

Many of the men expressed living in conditions with little to no positive interaction during their time of incarceration. Most days were spent in survival or self-protection mode, and because of the pressures of their living situations they developed negative attitudes and/or behaviors. The men implied that because of institutional financial woes, they felt those in the justice system were not anxious to deal with their emotional health unless they were showing severe life threatening health issues. The failure to address emotional health means these hidden emotions often show up through various symptoms of a person's life, their behaviors and even the crimes that led to arrest and conviction. Those who have been institutionalized often lack the emotional intelligence to identify, use, understand and manage their emotions. Our challenge was to assist the ex-offender in changing old patterns by making positive choices and decisions that are different from the path that got them involved in the criminal system. The project wasn't billed as a quick fix, believing that all of the participants could be treated for the same symptoms. We emphasized that each person would react differently to life issues based on race, culture and socioeconomic background.

Study and Methodology

Program Design

This book includes a discussion of the way the men created meaning in their lives living in a minimally supervised setting, awaiting reentry into society after existing a period of time in corrections and/or the prison system. The project also included determining the emotional response of these men in prior life events, positive and negative activities, family and other types of relationships. A narrative approach was applied to the study knowing that the realities for the participants selected are: 1) they have confessed a traditional belief in Christianity; 2) all are recovering from substance abuse and 3) all are living in the Community Transitional Housing for a minimum of seven days and no longer than 18 months awaiting expiration of their prison sentence. The narrative approach was determined to be the best because it captured stories and experiences through interviews with the men. It was thought to be a less biased way of approaching this non-traditional ministry context and social issue.[58] The process began with each man articulating his own personal stories and struggles as a way of naming the struggle and claiming the freedom by admitting past failures and shortcomings without judgment or retribution, a beginning of the progression toward transformation.

Subjects for the study came from participants of the Wednesday Night Bible Study. The program goals were explained in detail in addition to my role as pastor at St. Peter's United Church of Christ and as a Doctor of Ministry student at Louisville Presbyterian Seminary. Volunteers for participation in the program were encouraged following the sharing of this pertinent information about the program. The participants were asked to read and sign Informed Consent Forms (ICF) prior to beginning the project. The pre-analysis data was initially collected through interviews recorded through digital videography utilizing an electronic notebook. The interviews were less than 7 minutes per participant. Guided open-ended written questions were asked to glean the participant's responses and to obtain verbal data for the project. Notes were taken during the interview with a follow-up review of the videos for later use. The interviews and observations were also put into verbatim form for easy reading and reference. After reviewing all the material and becoming familiar with the individuals, similarities between the participants were identified and target questions for follow-up regarding their Christian belief system, family relationships and reasons for incarceration were explored. Verbal and visual data were gathered by observing the interactions of the participant in various individual and group settings.

The signed ICF's, research notes, verbatim and reflections were stored in electronic format in Microsoft Word, Excel and PDF format for further transcription and review. The videos were stored on DVD for future reference. All information was stored by the following categories: Lessons, Pre-videos, Project, Support Documents and Verbatim. An outside observer was present each week to validate the information taught, monitor evaluation collection and to write a weekly observation report.

The subject matter was selected based on emotions described during sacred conversations of pastoral care and also observations of information in video interviews. Primary emotions, those emotions that we feel first, as an initial response to a situation versus secondary emotions, meaning emotions that appear as a result of the primary emotions were reviewed to determine the order of the presentation of the weekly material. Materials were written and reviewed weekly to address concerns learned through discussions and class participation. The material plan was four pages or less and written on a 10th grade educational level based on historic educational level of those in the Russell community. Each participant was given their own copy of the material for review and reference at a later time if desired.

Activities and Resources to be used

The focus group convened each Wednesday at 7 pm. The sessions were opened with prayer followed by the introduction of each person to the group. The establishments of appropriate personal boundaries for interaction were addressed to the group as being instrumental in fostering dialogue of open communication and the creation of a safe environment where cultural differences and diversity are promoted. The study groups were maintained at no more than eight men. The purposes of the lessons were to assist the participant in discerning the appropriate emotional choices once they graduated from the in-house Substance Abuse Program and as they transitioned back into normal society. Following the initial interview, the participants returned to class weekly to participate in seven additional life skills modules on: depression, grief, anger, fear, positive relationships, marriage, and parenting; one module each week. The timeframe of each session was 90 minutes including 30-45 minutes of didactic teaching and 45 minutes of open discussion. Evaluation forms were completed at the conclusion of each session by the students and the official observer for further evaluation of the material and presentation methods.

The Opening Session - Introduction

In the opening session, the residents in attendance were given an overview of the life skills modules to be presented throughout the eight week course. The course would begin this session with a pre interview. Based on the make-up of the residents of the facility, it was not assumed that those interested in participating in the study were all Christians. Therefore the pre interview was an opportunity to identify a specific group of participants who expressed Christian beliefs and understanding.

This initial session included each participant being interviewed with a set of open-ended questions for determination of their belief system and how it had affected their background recounting personal historical events, their personal journey and experiences, and their understanding of God as it relates to life skills and spiritual formation. The interview questions were: 1. Are you a Christian? 2. What is your understanding of the Christian faith? 3. Were you raised in the church? What denomination? 4. When I mention the term life skills what do you think of? 5. Based on your knowledge of the bible, what does the bible teach us about the following emotions, gender identity and family activities and experiences such as: (1) grief (2) depression (3) anger (4) fear (5) sexuality (6) marriage and (7) parenting? 6. Please share with me your upbringing and involvement in the 7 life skills previously mentioned. The person being interviewed was separated from the remaining participants to allow for confidentiality in the conversation. The participants awaiting their interview time were encouraged to use their waiting time to fellowship and converse with the other participants. It was felt that the excitement of speaking from the heart[59] and for the opportunity to have unrestricted conversations of their life story was an incentive for them to continue in the program. The interviews were documented for review at the conclusion of the study.

Module 1 – Grief

The goals of the seven week life skills course were re-introduced to the class participants. The written lesson regarding grief was presented for 45 minutes, followed by 45 minutes of open discussion. Four phases of grief as outlined in the article "Dealing with Grief" were discussed by the participants. The phases of grief included: 1) Shock , the days and weeks immediately following a devastating loss, common feelings include numbness and unreality, like being trapped in a bad dream. 2) Reality, the loss taking hold, the setting up of deep sorrow, accompanied by weeping and other forms of emotional release. The occurrence of loneliness and depression was mentioned. 3)

Reaction, which may include anger, brought on by feelings of abandonment and helplessness, may be directed toward family, friends, doctors, the one who died or deserted us, or even God. Other typical feelings to be discussed included listlessness, apathy, and guilt over perceived failures or unresolved personal issues and, 4) Recovery, the gradual, almost imperceptible return to normalcy or time of adjustment to the new circumstances in life.[60] The scriptural text of Ezekiel 24:16-17 was used as an example of grief suppression. Personal narratives of the project leader were used as an opportunity to foster discussion with the participants regarding life experiences that may have caused times of grief in their own lives.

Module 2 – Depression

The previous lesson on grief was briefly reviewed and was introduced as one of the causes of depression. The lesson was presented for 45 minutes, followed by 45 minutes of open discussion. The lesson included practical definitions and terms of emotions along with several biblical scriptures to reinforce the type of emotion, and how it is addressed both positively and negatively in the bible. The four phases of depression discussed by the participants were: 1) Normal/Situational depression caused by normal problems of life such as a midlife crisis or empty nest syndrome. 2) Masked depression, buried and/or hidden conflicts that can be seen through excessive busyness and activities, addictions and other behaviors. 3) Neurotic depression or clinical depression and 4) Psychotic depression, a loss of reality. The scripture focus of the lesson was based on a bible series written by June Hunt, which centered on Jonah 4:3-9 and his rebellion against God as an example of normal/situational depression.[61] The lesson describes Jonah as being distraught because he did not want to follow God's instructions to help the Ninevites, for he did not deem them worthy of salvation. The situation that God had placed Jonah with the Ninevites, as prophet of God's and truth in word, caused him to flee and withdraw into a place of depression and sadness.

Module 3 – Anger

The previous lesson on depression was briefly reviewed. The written lesson was presented for 50 minutes, followed by open discussion. Due to the number of scriptures cited in the pamphlet, participants were asked to choose various scriptures for discussion. Following discussion, the participants were asked to complete a Self-Scoring Quiz on coping with anger to determine if any of them might need to seek additional support for anger issues. The lesson included practical definitions and terms on anger and biblical scriptures listed to reinforce the positive and negative use in the bible. We discussed the feeling of anger as a response to pain, both physical and psychological. There was a distinction established regarding anger as primary or secondary emotions based on feeling fear, being attacked, offended, disrespected, trapped or pressured. Other symptoms of anger, such as rapid speech, sarcasm or cynicism, revenge fantasies and drinking or using drugs were also reviewed.[62]

Module 4 –Fear

The previous lesson on anger was briefly reviewed. The written lesson regarding fear was presented for 45 minutes, followed by open discussion. Fear was discussed as a primary emotion that might trigger secondary emotions such as grief, depression and anger. Fear was addressed in this lesson as a primary emotion. Thus, if threatened, we may feel fear. When we hear of a death, we may feel sadness. The emotion of fear is unthinking, and a natural response. It was reiterated to the men that fear happens to all of us. Symptoms of fear were discussed, such as mild or extreme muscular tension, fainting, adrenalin rush, losing the content of our bowels, and phobias.

Module 5 - Positive Relationships

In the initial design, the focus of this module was sexuality. The focus of the module was changed to positive relationships, to reflect how we communicate with one another positively and negatively; which has a direct effect on relationships. The decision was made to change the focus of this module because I was the only female in the group and I did not want the topic of sexuality to distract from the safe environment that we created in previous weeks. This life skill module provided an opportunity to model positive relationships by working and interacting with one another through group exercises and interaction utilizing role play. Following the group exercise, the lessons on positive relationships were presented for 45 minutes, followed by open discussion. The scriptural focus for the lesson was taken from familiar biblical passages of Luke 10:27-37 and Ephesians 4:1-2; 25-29; 31-32. The lesson concluded with the meaning of personal boundaries and how it helps with our self-esteem and opinion of our self-worth.

Module 6 – Marriage

The previous session on positive relationships was reintroduced as we approached the topic of marriage. The lesson was presented for 45 minutes, followed by open discussion. Trust was discussed as the key ingredient to marriage. We discussed how trust is built through the establishment of appropriate personal boundaries for interaction, open communication and the creation of a safe and healthy environment for both individuals. Various scriptures were used as examples of healthy and unhealthy marriages.

Module 7 – Parenting

The session opened with a review of the written material for 30 minutes. The remaining time was designed for the class participants to work in pairs to analyze various case studies. The groups were allowed to pick from an envelope that had a total of ten cases. The groups had 15 minutes to discuss their case and write their answers on poster board for discussion by the entire group. The purpose of this lesson was for the participants to put into practice positive relationships and to determine their knowledge and use of the appropriate life skills taught using multiple sources of materials[63] and the instruction they received over the previous seven weeks. It was hoped the participant would learn to make better decisions as wise and informed parents. This final evaluation method was utilized because it provided a holistic view of life events of the participants, and it also gave the project leader an opportunity to examine the comprehension of the training activities, and for the men to apply their understanding of various materials to complex real-life situations.

Limitations

This study was limited to participants who indicated that they had an applied understanding of the Christian faith. It was expected that not all participants would complete the program due to parole violations or relocations to other facilities within or outside of the Russell community before the conclusion of the eight week program, which included the pre interview on week one and seven modules each week thereafter. Sessions could be relocated due to unforeseen building maintenance issues. Sessions could also be extended for several sessions due to police raids and other unknown security issues. Finally, the men were participating on a volunteer basis and were under no obligation to attend weekly sessions.

Expected Outcomes

It was anticipated that 50% of the participants would complete the program. Participants would be expected to complete at least 5 of 7 life-skills classes within an eight week period, and be able to demonstrate use of learned skills during role play and/or case study. Our times together were designed to foster trust and positive relationships among those participating, hoping that they would become a support group for each other during their time at CTS and after release to their respective communities. It was expected that the participants that completed the program would begin to contemplate and think about making positive life choices when released and feel less anxiety and fear about making independent, positive and healthy life choices once paroled and on their own. It was hoped that as life events arose, which may cause times of disappointment or rejection, that those who participated in the program would not allow these emotions to control their behavior or activities negatively. At a minimum the participants would have resources to assist in identifying the problem to obtain additional help and support if needed. Finally, it was expected that participants that remain in the Russell community will establish an ongoing relationship with St. Peter's faith community based on spiritual formation and their desire to continue in worship and mission work in the community, developing a spirit of volunteerism to give back to those who have nurtured and supported them during the transformation process. It was my goal to stay in contact with men released from the facility for at least 6 months to monitor changed behavior and progress toward successful reentry into the community.

112

CHAPTER FOUR

INTEPRETING THE LEARNING OF THE PROJECT

I have attempted, through this Christian Life Skills Project, to impart healthy life skills through modeling Christian behavior with the men hoping that at least half would adopt new behavior by recognizing and naming what needed to be changed in their lives and thinking and claiming how to make the changes permanently. After reviewing the interviews of the men, the data revealed that most of the men could define life skills; however, none had ever looked at life skills through a theological or scriptural framework. Yet, all had confessed to having a relationship with Jesus Christ and were raised in what they defined as Christian homes with good Christian morals and values.

This project also delivered another opportunity to provide the men with additional support that they may not receive from agencies that appear proficient in the traditional model of rehabilitation, but may not promote the spiritual insight in making the best choices once the individual is on their own. It is my hope that along with emotional healing, nurtured by spiritual understanding and guidance, the ex-offender will in time change their behavior. During this short period of time, the act of empowerment and the gift of nurturing have helped some of the men name their oppression, uplift one another through building fellowship and sacred and intimate conversation, actively participate in community, develop strategies and goals for personal progress and recognize the need for change so that they can socially re-engage family and society. Finally, because of the act of surrogacy within the church community, I believe the men could feel God's transforming power at work in their lives and those around them. It takes the entire village to work together to holistically provide life-long healing. It is my hope that, as a minister and pastor, this project will empower men and women to move beyond cultural expectations, to nurture and help resurrect the individuals from spiritually dead places.

The effectiveness of this program can be seen through the following theological reflections realized during the eight week course.

Module 1 – Grief

Theodore, age 40 seemed genuinely affected by the lesson and opened up during the time of discussion. Theodore, a decorated veteran had used drugs for about fifteen years. He was unable to keep employment because of the drugs. After being arrested multiple times, Theodore was given the option of participating in the state ordered Substance Abuse Program (SAP) or serve out a felony sentence at Luther Luckett Correctional facility. Theodore chose SAP and as a result of his choice ended up at the CTS. Theodore shared that one particular night while under the influence of drugs at home, his father went into distress from COPD (chronic obstructive pulmonary disease). Theodore admitted his mother had tried to call 911for EMS from the house phone but couldn't get a dial tone. Finally, she traced the phone line to his room and informed him that his Dad was in distress and that he needed medical help quickly. Unfortunately, Theodore's father died prior to the arrival of the ambulance. Theodore began to sabotage himself because of his grief and guilt. He was unable to cope with the reality of his participation in his father not getting the help he needed quickly, and his subsequent death. His father may have died anyway, but not knowing had fostered Theodore's guilt, resulting in increased drug use.

We determined through conversation that Theodore is probably in the recovery stage, a return to normalcy and perhaps it was time for him to draw on other professional and spiritual resources for guidance. It was shared that in general, in society men are told not to mourn, weep, cry or show any outward emotions in dealing with grief as outlined in Ezekiel 24:16-17. Yet, Theodore exposed his hurt and pain in what he considered a safe environment and was able to empty himself of feelings that he had bottled up for years. True transformation began when he was able to admit his imperfections and came to understand that God loves him through it all.

Module 2 – Depression

Depression was such a hot topic for the men. At the conclusion of the 90 minute class, one of the participants, Jim, age 23 raised his hand and asked for prayer from the group because he felt like he was depressed. His brother had died from drug use a couple days earlier and Jim was grieving because he hadn't been there for his brother or his mother who was now all alone. As Jim began to tell his story, he mentioned many conflicts within his family which appeared to be masked through his repeated drug use and attitude of helplessness. His mother was now drug free, but had overdosed on drugs several times throughout his short life and now his teenage brother was dead from drug use. He was concerned that his mother might turn back to drugs without his help.

    I had centered the lesson on Jonah 4:3-9 and his rebellion against God, however, I believe the Holy Spirit used the opportunity for this small group of men to learn how and show other men how to be compassionate and caring with one another. So many times it seems that preachers and teachers lesson plans are designed to teach one thing or another, however, God knows exactly what we are standing in need of and provides it at the right time. This particular lesson led to discussion regarding the meaning of belonging to Christ and the definition of unconditional love. The men expressed acts of compassion shown them and they to others, trying to make the connection to their faith and understanding of God. This time together promoted like-mindedness among the participants. "Then make me truly happy by agreeing wholeheartedly with each other, loving one another, and working together with one mind and purpose" (Philippians 2:1, Message).

During this lesson the men truly revealed the attitude of Christ in dealing with Jim. Nothing was said to intentionally move the men in this direction, it was a spontaneous reaction which truly reflects the spontaneity of life. We must be adaptable through life's journey. Several of the participants commented on the level of intimacy experienced during this particular lesson.

Module 3 – Anger

One of the outside observers, John, approximately 50 years old, expressed to the group that he dealt with anger by laughing things off. John, an African American, described himself as a successful business man and an active church leader and participant. The initial reactions by the group regarding his comments were mixed. Laughter for John was a survival tool and the way he learned to cope with the emotion of anger was expressed through the symptoms of laughter. As John shared with the group, he described that as a young boy, he witnessed his Dad beat his Mom. John indicated he would get so angry at the abuse, but he was too small to do anything about it. He had even tried to get his father to stop the abuse, but when he spoke to him, his father threatened to beat him too. So, to deal with the violence he just started laughing to cope with the pain and continues to do the same now to control his anger.

Unfortunately, even as a grown man, it appears he is still unable to deal with anger in a healthy manner. To laugh or smile through the emotion as an adult seemed to be an avoidance mechanism, instead of confronting the issues that caused the underlying emotion. This discussion on anger seemed to provoke an emotion in John and provided him an opportunity to express his feelings in a safe place. John had only come to observe, not participate, but the opportunity and discussion provided the opening to express unresolved feelings. Even though the other participants did not necessarily agree with his coping methods, they were supportive of him in their comments. Many expressed issues of abuse in their own lives and indicated that they too had come up with their own coping mechanisms. Unfortunately, for the majority in this session, drugs and alcohol became the primary way to cope, which led them to addiction and a period of incarceration. John reminded us of the scriptures, "People leave this world no better off than when they came. All their hard work is for nothing like working for the wind. Throughout their lives, they live under a cloud--frustrated, discouraged, and angry" (Ecclesiastes 5:16 18, NLT).

When I think of this passage, it reminds me of the Peanuts character Linus who always seemed to have a cloud of dirt over his head. Linus was so filthy that the dirt hovered over him no matter where he went. I think this passage speaks directly to John. Even though he had come to be successful in some circles, he appeared to live under a cloud because of the way he continues to deal with anger. Avoidance or not dealing with anger directly for him is better than naming it. Mental health defines this as passive aggressive and I would hope that being in a safe environment with others who are dealing with this emotion will provide him with an opportunity to move from under the cloud. Unfortunately, John never returned again as an observer, I believe, continuing the habit of avoidance.

Module 4 –Fear

This module helped two men participating in the SAP to express the emotion of fear; Jim an intravenous drug user and Ted, an alcoholic. Jim and Ted expressed that the fear of death and not being there for family had caused both to want to change. They had begun a life of substance abuse to cope with low self-esteem and a negative cultural environment. They were willing to admit that they were afraid at different times in their lives. I believe positive fear is what caused both men to move them from complacency in life into action. Jim and Ted discussed how being part of the SAP program has helped them both to change their life and their willingness to share that fear with others. I believe these sessions could be instrumental in helping others to overcome their fears. In addition, they rededicated their life to Christ while actively participating in church life at St. Peters UCC, and feel this is essential to their future. "No, dear brothers and sisters, I have not achieved it,[a] but I focus on this one thing: Forgetting the past and looking forward to what lies ahead, I press on to reach the end of the race and receive the heavenly prize for which God, through Christ Jesus, is calling us" (Philippians 3:13-14). Paul teaches us in this text that we all have a past that we can allow to keep us in bondage. However, because Christ Jesus died on the cross for our sins, because I now seek to be in relationship with God through my acceptance of Christ that I now can look forward to a rewarding future. Jim and Ted have expressed that their renewed relationship with Christ has helped them to deal with their past and they are hopeful for a life now free from crime and drug use.

Module 5 - Positive Relationships

The lesson focused on the familiar biblical passages of Luke 10:27-37 and Ephesians 4:1-2; 25-29; 31-32, in which they all seemed to understand the teaching of love your neighbor as yourself and being like Christ, being humble and gentle in how we deal with one another. However, loving self appears to be the real issue for many of the residents. The lesson concluded with us striving to treat others the way we want to be treated and because there are times we do not treat ourselves well, that reflects on how we see our own self-worth. Personal boundaries help with our self-esteem and opinion of our self-worth.

Donald P. Smith tells us first that self-esteem is a function, not of what we are born with, but of how we use our consciousness—the choices we make concerning awareness, the honesty of our relationship to reality, and the level of our personal integrity. God's grace builds self-esteem which is the essence of the gospel. In Jesus Christ, God forgives our guilt and accepts us as we are. When we respond to God's forgiving love and acceptance, God frees us to accept ourselves as we are.[64]

As we learn to love ourselves, then it will become easier to be more loving to those around us. We will interact better with those around us and treat them with respect. We should have Christ-like principles for our lives, our homes and in any setting that we live, work or play.

Module 6 – Marriage

Many of the residents focused on Ephesians 5:23-28 that the man is the head of his wife. They had learned or heard it at some point in their upbringing and literally tried to model this scripture in their lives. A few admitted they felt this passage was intended for them to control their wife through both verbal and/or forced submissiveness. Therefore, a lot of time was spent on how to love and honor self and wife/partner just as we love and honor Christ. We also discussed being married to an unbeliever, the role in marriage and marriage as a covenant.

There was tremendous energy and honesty during this lesson, reflective of the safe environment. Many of the men admitted to having affairs throughout their marriages and the lack of honoring their covenant of marriage. Several admitted their relationship was not love but lust. Some expressed that they felt as though they would never be in a lasting marriage again because of their past behaviors.

There was a powerful move of the Holy Spirit during this session. Many of the residents responded about adulterous relationships expressing being sorrowful and the desire to change their behavior. There was an impromptu time of prayer for repentance and God's forgiveness. Another opportunity to offer hope and encouragement came when one of the residents expressed that he didn't feel as though God could ever forgive him for the things he had done to himself and others. During this time of discussion the lesson was diverted from marriage in the human sense to the biblical sense of our marriage to Christ. There was also discussion of God's saving grace toward each of us. We were reminded that when we ask for God's forgiveness and repent of our sins, God is quick to forgive us. The hardest step is for us to forgive ourselves. We also talked about overcoming addictions and becoming conquerors because of being in Christ Jesus based on Romans 8:31-39.

    Once again God provided opportunities for healing in several areas. It was also important to recognize that despite my best laid plans, the Holy Spirit was leading the class to a place of repentance and reconciliation with God and others.

Module 7 – Parenting

The format of this lesson changed and class was started with the residents and observers working in two's on various case studies. The groups were allowed to pick from an envelope that had a total of ten cases. They worked in groups for 15 minutes to discuss their case and then were asked to write their answers on poster board for discussion by the entire group. The purpose of this lesson was for the participants to put into practice positive relationships and to determine their knowledge and use of the life skills taught over the past seven weeks in making decisions as wise and informed parents. It was determined that they all had gained a broader knowledge of the grief, depression, anger, fear, positive relationships, marriage, and parenting skills. However, the difficult part would be putting what they have learned into practice on a regular basis.

Observer Reflections

The independent observer was a 42 year old male named Timothy, an active church participant, married, father raising a daughter under joint custody arrangements and an ex-offender. He has been out of jail for over 20 years. He stated in his evaluations that discussions were in-depth with great interaction with the instructor and the participants. "After each introduction Pastor J inserted a brief story of her own experiences with the topic of discussion, thus allowing the participants a glimpse into her personal life." This transparency drew the participants into discussion with the sense of connecting. Several meetings tripled in number from the initial meeting. There were a lot of useful, meaningful conversations going on in the sessions, such as one participant who spoke of his depression and his battles on a daily basis. He was received by Pastor J with her understanding and by his peers, one of which offered himself as a person he could talk with when he needed a listening ear.

By the completion of the seventh lesson, a few of the participants shared with the observer how these lessons had moved them to seek help from doctors and other health professionals that may be able to help them dig deeper into their situations and emotions.
Other observation remarks included that the participants did better when they had more discussion time and less didactic material. Discussion appeared to bring about a better understanding of the subject matter.

Methods of Evaluation

Seven modules were written to support the curriculum based on information obtained from professional journals and periodicals and the Christian

Bible, showing documented knowledge and research of the prison population, reentry and recidivism in an urban community. After each module was completed participants voluntarily completed evaluation forms pertaining to each individual session. The average age throughout was 48.2 years of age; 98.6% of those attending felt the information should be a resource for the future development of a community wide Christian Life Skills Program. 99.2% of those attending felt the materials were an effective part of the lessons, and 96.1% of those attending had never participated in the corresponding lessons prior to attending.

Statistical Test 1

To examine the relationship between usefulness of the materials and presentation (delivery) of the material, the Spearman Rho test was utilized. The results show significant relationship exists between usefulness of the material and presentation of the material (r=.174, p< .05); therefore the null hypothesis was rejected.

Statistical Test 2

To examine the difference between overall satisfaction total and identifying race; the Mann Whitney-U test was utilized. The results show no significance between satisfaction total and race (z=.-843, p>.05); therefore the null hypothesis was accepted.

Statistical Test 3

To examine the relationship between all seven modules and overall satisfaction total; the Mann Whitney-U test was utilized. The results showed a significant relationship existed between all seven modules and overall satisfaction (r2= .731 = 53.4(moderate), p<.05); therefore the null hypothesis was accepted.

Qualitative Stats

Qualitative themes throughout all seven modules were centered on how the Bible guides, directs, and instructs (empowers) individuals struggling with certain issues; communication; love; trust; expression; and accountability (Grief, Depression, Anger, Fear, Positive Relationships, Marriage, and Parenting).

A Few Notes on the Test[65]

The Mann Whitney-U and Spearman Rho are statistical tests that are non-parametric deeming them more suitable for sample bases lower than 25 but not greater than 250. Each test included two variables in combination of 1) Nominal independent variables (IV) and ordinal dependent variables (DV) for the Mann Whitney-U and ordinal DVs for the Spearman Rho. The Mann-Whitney U test measures differences between groups whereas the Spearman Rho test measured relationships.

Summary

Although seven men had actually agreed to participate in the research project, the breakdown of actual participants over the 8 weeks was an average of 13 men per module. The high was 24 participants in the lesson on anger; and the low was four on the final discussion on parenting. Much of the fluctuation in attendance was attributed to men completing their program and receiving release for home placement. Of the participants the average racial breakdown was 38% African American and 62% Euro-American decent. The ages ranged from 18 through 55; with the highest age group being ages 41-50.

As we worked with the men over the 8 week period, we discovered that some of them were attending the class as a distraction from the daily routine of the facility. Others stopped participating because the subject matter was too personal and they were unwilling to expose themselves to the men they lived with and to outsiders. There were a few who despite our wanting the best for them were unwilling to receive the nurture and support offered by a church organization and a female pastor.

For some of these men who were completing long-term prison sentences, they had come to realize the opportunities they had missed or lost by being incarcerated. Plus, others had expressed renewing their relationship with Christ while incarcerated had made a difference in their outlook on life and they were looking at this program as an opportunity toward having a new chance for life. However, only four men completed the program and were deemed to be able to contemplate healthy choices as evidenced by the case studies that were completed in module seven. These four men also used their participation in the program as further evidence to the CTS officials of their determination to change their lives and behaviors, and as a result were allowed to provide weekly volunteer service at the church.

Unfortunately, there is little evidence of real transformation because of the transient nature of the men in the project. There was no incentive beyond self-will for the men to go further in dealing with their emotional health beyond this 8 week project. According to various Stages of Change Theory, people go through five main stages as they identify the need for different behavior, then learn and adopt new behavior. These five main stages of change are as follows: 1) the person has not thought about making behavior change, 2) the person begins to think about making a change, 3) the person prepares for change, 4) the person begins to make changes, 5) the person continues to perform the new behavior two to three year period after the change begins.[66] The culture of this transitional facility only allowed the individual participants to begin to think about making changes in their lives in these respective areas. Emotional transformation for the men, I feel will become secondary concerns for them once they are released from CTS; taking a backseat to their basic daily needs such as adequate housing, employment and traditional re-entry support groups within and outside the Russell community.

CHAPTER FIVE

IMPLICATIONS OF LEARNING FOR FUTURE PRACTICE

Revised Goals and Rationale

The goals of the learning project were developed with the idea that in eight weeks some of the participants would be able to make positive life decisions based on the lessons. However, adjustments in the goals were made throughout the project because of several uncontrolled forces within the facility such as inmate parole violations and/or early release from the program. In addition, because this project was made part of the weekly Men's Bible Study, the number of participants could not be limited. Several sessions turned into group pastoral care sessions, using the various emotional topics as opportunities for discussion, spiritual direction and life application.

As a result, the project became more of an opportunity to provide ongoing pastoral care to the men, establish a church Watch Care relationship with the men until they are permanently released from CTS, and to provide referrals to other facilities based on the individual needs of the person. Christie Neuger in the book, *The Care of Men*, shared that pastors who had men's groups organized around support, spiritually, or mix of study and support, found that they knew a lot about the men in those groups and that the men were more likely to come to the pastor directly in time of need. Those groups also created supportive relationships among the men that functioned outside of the group structure itself.[67] Since the start of this program and my involvement with the men through a pastoral care relationship, over 60 men have participated in various phases of the program and many have become Watch Care members at St. Peter's UCC.

Despite the program taking on a different shape than originally planned, the Christian Life Skills Program continues to be taught quarterly at CTS and has been since January 2012. Some of the handouts were re-worked to strengthen the reference material. Also, a second class has been added at the church to support female ex-offenders that are a part of the St. Peter's faith community. In 2012, the lessons were introduced to the St. Peter's faith community by way of intergenerational group Bible Study and a total of 20 men and 23 women have completed the course. In addition, because of the promotion of the program through word of mouth of several CTS participants and referrals from the Healing Place and Alcoholic Anonymous, the program is now part of a platform of holistic family support and nurturing, addressing the unique needs of youth, women, men, ex-offenders and the aging through the St. Peter's Molo Village Community Development Corporation (MVCDC).

In the continuing development of the MVCDC, several segments of the village will play a crucial role in dealing with incarcerated men and women who are released from correctional institutions. This will remain a primary focus for the village, as we offer ministries and mission to those with criminal background, but programs will also be extended to family members affected by a cycle of criminal behavior. In the book Prison & Slavery, statistics reveal that over half of released prisoners have a problem staying out of trouble in the first three years of their new freedom; many do not make it six months. Unfortunately, the trend is that most released inmates wind up back in trouble, jail, or prison because they are unable to cope in the free world. Many parolees commit new crimes and are returned to prison.[68] Then, the destruction of the family unit is a major concern. Juvenile delinquency and crime are directly linked to poverty.

> Youth from father-absent households, especially those who never had a father in the household, have significantly higher incarceration rates. A 2002 survey of jail inmates showed 39% lived in mother-only households. About 46% of jail inmates in 2002 had a previously incarcerated family member, and 20% experienced a father in prison or jail. Incarceration accelerates the destruction of the American family. About 1.5 million children have incarcerated parents.[69]

Based on these numbers, we are preparing ministry and mission to address many of these areas of concerns. It is believed that successful reentry programs must include more than supplying housing, but programs must take up a holistic approach providing a support network for both those re-engaging public society and their family members. According to the Maryland Reentry Partnership Initiative, the most effective way to help stem recidivism is to bring all of these programs under one roof. The ultimate vision of the mission is about remolding a crime-battered life of individuals, the prevention of recidivism and also the healing of the family life unit that is often plagued in a cyclical pattern of crime, from the infant up to the adult.

MVCDC will continue to offer Christian life-skills coaching and mentoring, as we partner with other agencies for traditional life-skill courses and job placement programming. The MVCDC program will be modeled after the highly successful re-entry program called the Heaven's Gates Employment of California, which provides effective adult models and examples for children and youth. They have found that many times these children and youth are copying the adult lives of those cycling through prison. The curriculum for that program includes Academies Consortium, vocational training, mentoring, therapies, tutoring, life-skills, and employment.[70] The MVCDC will explore all these areas for inclusion at the village.

Theological Reflection on Outcomes

As a 21st Century Mission within a Black Church, we will continue to emphasize the values of family relationships, parental care, self and self-sacrificing concern for others, sharing, and hospitality. Homer Ashby describes this as a unitary view of society, meaning that what one member of a group does has ramifications on all members of society.[71] There is no individual action that does not incorporate consequences. Therefore, as a community, we are interconnected and must help one another in order to incorporate consequences to have a positive outcome. We must stress this connectedness if we are to combat family disruption and poverty among African American and poor families.

Robert London Smith, Jr., prompts us as the church, in *From Strength to Strength: Shaping a Black Practical Theology for the 21st Century* to deal with the modern black and urban community. Also, Smith helps us to evaluate our mission and legacy as we face an excess of new challenges including institutional slavery, discrimination in housing, employment, medical care, education and legal matters including law enforcement issues. Smith tells us that it is imperative that all churches begin to evaluate their missions to determine how to deal with these issues in a more diverse and disadvantaged society.[72] Karen Labacqz further reminds us that good spiritual care of congregations does not happen simply by attending to personal issues presented in individual pastoral counseling or to institutional issues presented by the local congregation; it demands a larger social critique that focuses on societal levels of injustice that cause suffering for many and distorts the perspectives and lives of all.[73] We, as the church, must show the people of this world the truth about God's justice and help empower all people to live out Gods purpose for their lives.

The need for this program became a reality as we saw this love and compassion transform the behaviors and outlook of the participants. However, we rejoice in the story of Norman, a resident of CTS who came to the church, sat in the back alone for several weeks before interacting with others within the congregation. His discomfort was painfully noticeable most often through the times of congregational fellowship. However, during times of pastoral care I discovered that fear kept him from sitting with the other church participants. Norman indicated he had been imprisoned for 30 years and feared being in contact with others. The freedom to engage in simple conversation with others without retribution seemed daunting for this middle age man. Norman felt like he did not know how to have regular conversations with others. In addition, he showed tremendous nervousness during social interaction, whether it was altar call or "passing of the peace." He attributed the anxiety to his learning through long-term institutional life; "don't communicate unless told, no personal contact and follow orders." Yet, because of his renewed faith in God, he felt compelled to participate in worship and be among people who were welcoming to him despite his past. The Christian Life Skills course enabled him to express his emotions, and through our partnership with other agencies, where able to get him an adequate job and housing.

Implications for Further Research

Several funding opportunities have been awarded to the MVCDC for support of men reentering society from the penal system. In 2012, the United Church of Christ Indiana Kentucky Conference Social Action Committee awarded the MVCDC funds to support the Christian Life Program at CTS for one year. This grant covered the publication cost and materials of the mini booklets used in class. Local governmental agencies have also shown interest in the program design and current levels of participation.

The MVCDC has also established a program that enrolled fifteen ex-offender participants in a 12 month holistic program, and another program involving 100 involving semi-annual Life skills workshops for offenders pending release. Participants are referred to the program through other partners and agencies. The scope of the MVCDC is broad; however, funding for this project is being specifically designed to supplement programs of mentoring, therapies, tutoring, life-skills and volunteerism.

We will assist and advocate with persons and caregivers through the planning and delivery of services by a highly effective staff in partnership with public and private organizations. Currently, MVCDC has four clergy who are trained in pastoral care and Christian Life Skills. Volunteers are used for basic educational skills tutoring, instruction materials preparation and assimilation for workshops, weekly therapies and mentoring sessions. Other trained clergy and facilitators will be added as the program is expanded. Services will be provided with respect, care and accountability for the good of the community. This will include the intentional helping of the participants to interpret the situation in which they live and to recognize and identify, specifically, how they are being hurt in society.

The measurable outcome/benefit for those participating in the revised program is that those enrolled participants in the 12 month program will show changed behavior through improved self-esteem, and increased interest in education either through obtaining GED or seeking higher education opportunities. Enrolled participants will volunteer 4-8 hours per week during the enrollment period, thus demonstrating a willingness to show compassion and help to others. Participants will complete at least 5 of 7 life-skills classes within a seven week period. At the conclusion of the program, participants will be able to demonstrate use of learned skills during role play and case study. The success of the program will be determined through a) Enrolled participant case notes, tracking sheets, certificate of course completion, progress and achievement plan and, b) Life-skills workshop certificate of course completion and job placement and retention.

Sustainability of the program is based on the premise that "it takes a village to raise a child." Therefore, it takes many partnerships and collaborations to affect change in our communities. The MVCDC will highlight areas of need and by supporting, educating and empowering our clients to become self-sufficient. Participants will be empowered to become productive members of society in which the whole community benefits. We have solicited support for the initial program through a patchwork of funding from the national and local churches of The United Church of Christ, in-kind donations from the community, and corporate and individual sponsorship. Also, an annual fundraising event, the Molo

Village Community Festival which features rides, health and educational booths for the community, will support the project. Clients will be charged a co-pay or small fee for various services to offset costs. Community events such as workshops and mini-conferences will be held annually to encourage community and civic support.

Preliminary discussions with leaders at the local university and medical school have begun for increased partnership with allied health and women's support services. These collaborations are seen as important parts of community infrastructure, serving several functions, including acting as a bridge between local residents, the community and public institutions, recognizing the need for joint solutions to many of these systemic issues.

The MVCDC will continue to leverage and collaborate with our current community resources such as: St. Peter's United Church of Christ, Community

Transitional Housing, and Mission Behind Bars and Beyond, Allied Health and Education (AHEC), The Center for Health Equity, Baptist Fellowship Center, and Dare to Care. This is an opportunity for us to broaden the programmatic thrust of the project to include all adult individuals within the Russell community. Cheryl Sanders reminds us that the church itself can be understood as the principal arena in which empowered individuals, families, and communities can devote their gifts and resources to serving the needs of others, consistent with the example of Jesus Christ.[74] The Molo Village CDC has become the arena as it provides services to individuals through five hamlets (divisions), while applying a holistic approach to addressing the needs of the individual and their family unit within the Russell community. Currently, there are three divisions that are up and running as a direct result of this project. First, "The Restored Village," which includes all things recovery and restoration: AA, Ex-Offenders (male, female and youth), and life skills. The 3 Alcoholic Anonymous groups housed at St. Peter's now are part of the Restored Village. Christian Life skills continue to be taught at both St. Peters and Community Transitional Housing. As a part of this program, both male and female offenders must complete community service. They will be also referred to the counseling center for life skills, goal setting and a transition plan. During transition they will complete four courses. Another village is "The Healthy Village," which includes all things health, including "Molo Health Care and Counseling Center." In this small village there are opportunities for exercise, health and nutrition classes, workshops and information, meal preparation instruction, The Healthy Village Garden, and Health Fairs and Screenings. A goal for 2015 will be to open a Health Clinic. The third village is "The Empowered Village," which is all things social justice and advocacy, education and employment for individuals and family. The Empowered Village teaches and encourages participants to find their voice and to stand against injustices and systems that seek to oppress them as people in a constructive and effective way. Issues will be raised and actions will be planned and executed. GED and higher education will be encouraged. Mentors will be made available to assist in studying for GED classes and assisting in college or trade school planning. Other villages planned for the future are: "The Future Village" and "The Isiduko Village." The Future Village will consist of children and youth development and mentoring programs. The Future Village will include a computer lab and library for doing homework. Mentors will be available to be matched with students with parental consent. The Isiduko Village will consist of senior adult programs. The Isiduko Village partners senior adults with other adults and children to listen to the stories of "old," share wisdom and provide mentorship. Senior adults are encouraged to volunteer and continue to use their skills and abilities to help build a healthy and compassionate village.

As a center of transformation and a place where family cares for each other, the village has become a Christian institution where we live out the model of love and compassion as spoken by Jesus in Matthew 25: 34-36 (Message). "I was hungry and you fed me, I was thirsty and you gave me a drink, I was homeless and you gave me a room, I was shivering and you gave me clothes, I was sick and you stopped to visit, I was in prison and you came to me." This is the real meaning of community and the overarching vision of the village, and despite not achieving the initial goal of the project; we have achieved so much more. We have restored a Russell Village.

APPENDIX A

DEFINITIONS

Alcoholic Anonymous - a fellowship of men and women who share their experience, strength and hope with each other that they may solve their common problem and help others to recover from alcoholism.
(http://www.aa.org/subpage.cfm)

Digital Storytelling - mixture of computer-based images, text, recorded audio narration, video clips and/or music.

Community Transitional Services - a 300 resident halfway house in Louisville Kentucky for men leaving the prison system.

Center for Disease Control - The CDC is one of the major operating components of the
Department of Health and Human Services. CDC's
Mission is to collaborate to create the expertise, information, and tools that people and communities need to protect their health – through health promotion, prevention of disease, injury and disability, and preparedness for new health threats.
(http://www.cdc.gov/about/organization/cio.htm)

Dare to Care - a member food bank of Feeding America that distributes food in the Kentuckian area.

Feeding America - a network of member food banks that distribute 3 billion pounds of food each year nationwide. (https://secure.feedingamerica.org/)

Holistic - the treatment of the whole person, taking into account mental and social factors, rather than just the physical symptoms of a behavior.

Institutionalized slavery - those forces that maintain second class citizenship through imposed oppression and other negative conditions against groups based on race and culture.

Mission Behind Bars and Beyond - a Christian led re-entry and life skills program formed to reconnect formerly incarcerated persons with positive community role models to assist in their transition from prison to community, thereby reducing recidivism and demonstrates an important role in walking with those leaving prisons.

Spiritual Direction – an opportunity to reflect intentionally on one's relationship with God in the presence of another who listens with compassion. (Lebacqz 2000)

Spiritual Formation – forming and shaping the Christian community in their faith and learning through scriptures what it means to be people of God.

Transformative Justice – to dramatically reduce the reliance on arrest, detention, and incarceration for addressing crime and to instead promote the use of restorative and transformative practices, relying on community-based alternatives as well as holistic alternatives.

APPENDIX B

PRE-INTERVIEW QUESTIONS

Rev. Jamesetta Ferguson
St. Peter's United Church of Christ
Louisville Presbyterian Seminary Doctorate of Ministry Program
Christian Life Skills Project

1. Are you a Christian?

2. What is your understanding of the Christian faith?

3. Were you raised in the church? What denomination?

4. When I mention the term life skills what do you think of?

5. Based on your knowledge of the bible, what does the bible teach us about the following life skills (1) grief (2) depression (3) anger (4) fear (5) relationship (6) marriage and (7) parenting?

6. Will you share with me your upbringing and involvement in these 7 life skills previously mentioned.

APPENDIX C

INFORMED CONSENT FORM FOR ST. PETERS UNITED CHURCH OF CHRIST – LIFE SKILLS COACHING

This informed consent form is for research to be held by Rev. Jamesetta Ferguson and the St. Peter's United Church of Christ. We are inviting you to participate in research titled, "Christian Life Skills Coaching."

Rev. Jamesetta Ferguson
St. Peter's United Church of Christ
Louisville Presbyterian Seminary Doctorate of Ministry Program

This Informed Consent Form has two parts:

• **Information Sheet** (to share information about the study with you)
• **Certificate of Consent** (for signatures if you choose to participate

You will be given a copy of the full Informed Consent Form

Part I: Information Sheet

Introduction
I am Rev. Jamesetta Ferguson, Senior Pastor of St. Peter's United Church of Christ. I am doing research on small group sessions designed to develop and enhance personal, interpersonal life skill choices for ex-offenders in re-entry

programs. I am going to give you information and invite you to be part of this research. You do not have to decide today whether or not you will participate in the research. Before you decide, you can talk to anyone you feel comfortable with about the research.

This consent form may contain words that you do not understand. Please ask me to stop as we go through the information and I will take time to explain. If you have questions later, you can ask them of me or of another researcher.)

Purpose of the research

The content of the course will focus on the seven areas of life skills coaching using biblical principles. The sessions will also provide each participant an opportunity to reflect on their understanding and use of life skills based on their biblical understanding.

Type of Research Intervention

This research will involve your participation in a 5 minute pre and post interview video recording of your religious upbringing and life experiences. Each participant will participate in seven group discussions that will take about 90 minutes each. The discussion topics will cover (1) grief (2) depression (3) anger (4) fear (5) sexuality (6) marriage and (7) parenting utilizing a biblical framework as the main point of reference.

Participant Selection

You are being invited to take part in this research because I feel that your experience as an ex-offender in the justice system can contribute much to our understanding and knowledge of local re-entry programs.

Voluntary Participation
Your participation in this research is entirely voluntary. It is your choice whether to participate or not. If you choose not to participate all the services you receive at St. Peter's UCC will continue and nothing will change.

Procedures
The format of the research study will include:
1. *Pre-interview (5 minutes) – week 1*
2. *Life Skills Coaching (90 minutes each) – week 2-7*
3. *Post-interview (5 minutes) – week 8*

(For Pre and Post Interviews)
Participate in an interview with Rev. Jamesetta Ferguson. During the interview, I will sit down with you in a comfortable place at Community Transitional Services or St. Peter's United Church of Christ. If you do not wish to answer any of the questions during the interview, you may say so and the interviewer will move on to the next question. No one else but the interviewer will be present unless you would like someone else to be there. The information recorded is confidential, and no one else except Rev. Jamesetta Ferguson will have access to the information documented during your interview. The entire interview will be tape-recorded, but no-one will be identified by name on the tape. The information recorded is confidential, and no one else except Rev. Jamesetta Ferguson will have access to the tapes.

(For group discussions)
You will take part in a discussion with 7-8 other persons with similar experiences. This discussion will be guided by Rev. Jamesetta Ferguson. The group discussion will start with me making sure that you are comfortable. I will also answer questions about the research that you might have. Then I might ask you questions about the life skills and give you time to share your knowledge. The questions will be about life skills in your community.

I will also talk about life skill practices more generally because this will give us a chance to understand more about life skills but in a different way. ***I will ask you to share personal beliefs, practices or stories, but you do not have to share any knowledge that you are not comfortable sharing.*** *The discussion will take place in Community Transitional Services or St. Peter's United Church of Christ., and no one else but the people who take part in the discussion and guide or myself will be present during this discussion.*
     Duration
The research takes place over 8 weeks in total. During that time, I will visit you two times for interviewing and 6 times for life skills coaching and each coaching session will last for about 90 minutes each.

Risks
I am asking you to share with me some very personal and confidential information, and you may feel uncomfortable talking about some of the topics. You do not have to answer any question or take part in the discussion/interview/survey if you don't wish to do so, and that is also fine. You do not have to give us any reason for not responding to any question or for refusing to take part in the interview.

Benefits
There will be no direct benefit to you, but your participation is likely to help us find out more about how to provide life skills coaching within our community.

Reimbursements

You will not be provided any financial incentive to take part in the research.

Confidentiality
The research being done St. Peter's United Church of Christ may draw attention and if you participate you may be asked questions by other people in the community. We will not be sharing information about you to anyone outside of the research team. The information that we collect from this research project will be kept private. Any information about you will have a number on it instead of your name. Only the researcher will know what your number is and we will lock that information up with a lock and key. It will not be shared with or given to anyone.

Part II: Certificate of Consent
(This section is mandatory)

I have read the foregoing information, or it has been read to me. I have had the opportunity to ask questions about it and any questions I have been asked have been answered to my satisfaction. I consent voluntarily to be a participant in this study

Print Name of Participant_____

Signature of Participant _____
Date _____
Day/month/year

If illiterate [75]
I have witnessed the accurate reading of the consent form to the potential participant, and the individual has had the opportunity to ask questions. I confirm that the individual has given consent freely.

Print name of witness_____
        Thumb print of participant
Signature of witness _____
Date _____
        Day/month/year

Statement by the researcher/person taking consent

I have accurately read out the information sheet to the potential participant, and to the best of my ability made sure that the participant understands that the following will be done:

1. *Pre-interview (5 minutes) – week 1*
2. *Life Skills Coaching (90 minutes each) – week 2-7*
3. *Post-interview (5 minutes) – week 8*

I confirm that the participant was given an opportunity to ask questions about the study, and all the questions asked by the participant have been answered correctly and to the best of my ability. I confirm that the individual has not been coerced into giving consent, and the consent has been given freely and voluntarily.

A copy of this ICF has been provided to the participant. Print Name of Researcher/person taking the consent_____

Signature of Researcher /person taking the consent_____

Date _____
             Day/month/year

APPENDIX D

Life Skills Coaching From A Pastoral Care Perspective

Lesson One – Grief

Rev. Jamesetta Ferguson - DMin Project
St. Peter's United Church of Christ
July 20, 2011

Content

The lessons will be taught in small groups of 6-8 people in a 90 minute timeframe. The participants are all ex-offenders transitioning from Department of Corrections back into their local communities as strong productive citizens. The timeframe will include 30-45 minutes of didactic teaching and 45 minutes of open discussion.

Introduction

Grief is an emotion that is often masked in multiple layers of appearances. Whenever we face loss, we experience grief and none of us deals with grief the same way. Each person reacts differently based on race, culture and social economic background. But we all experience this emotion on some level. Because grief has different appearances, it may affect our judgment in how we deal with the world around us and influence the choices that we make on a daily basis. Grief can even cause us in some instances to sabotage ourselves.

For some, the experience of grief may be physical: aches and pains, difficulty eating or sleeping or fatigue. We may constantly think of the person, even replaying in our mind some final episode or experience. Grief can affect our spiritual selves. We may struggle to find meaning in our loss; our relationship with God may change.[76]

During this lesson of Christian Life Skills Coaching, we will reflect on several biblical scriptures that reflect positively and some not so positively on grief. These scriptures, I feel are useful and meaningful resources for putting our emotions of grief in a proper perspective for everyday living.

Types of Grief

There are various types of grief which include: broken relationships, loss of pets, loss of jobs/employment, divorce, health and/or retirement. There are many other types of grief and it is important to remember that this emotion is defined as a loss to you individually.

At the age of twenty-two, 6 months after my first child was born, my father found out he had terminal cancer and was expected to live only 90 days longer. The period of grief began with that diagnosis and lasted for up to ten years. I had just reestablished a loving relationship with my father and was anxious for that father/daughter relationship, but also for my daughter to know her grandfather. His illness affected me physically from watching his health rapidly decline from the cancer, but also in knowing that he would soon not be with us. At first I struggled with how I was feeling, being teary eyed and sad at the mention of his name. However, these unpredictable emotions eventually went away.

This journey through grief has four phases[77]:

• Shock – In the days and weeks immediately following a devastating loss, common feelings include numbness and unreality, like being trapped in a bad dream.

• Reality – As the fact of the loss takes hold, deep sorrow sets in, accompanied by weeping and other forms of emotional release. Loneliness and depression may also occur.

• Reaction – Anger, brought on by feelings of abandonment and helplessness, may be directed toward family, friends, doctors, the one who died or deserted us, or even God. Other typical feelings include listlessness, apathy, and guilt over perceived failures or unresolved personal issues.

- Recovery – Finally, there is a gradual, almost imperceptible return to normalcy. This is a time of adjustment to the new circumstances in life.

Many times in dealing with grief, the key to overcoming grief is to first recognize that you are grieving. It is important to figure out how you have handled grief in the past and draw on other resources such as professional and spiritual for guidance.

Let us take a look at 2-3 ways in which the bible discusses grief.

- **Genesis 34:2** When Shechem son of Hamor the Hivite, prince of the region, saw her, he seized her and lay with her by force. (NRS) **Genesis 34:7** just as the sons of Jacob came in from the field. When they heard of it, the men were indignant and very angry (KJV –grief), because he had committed an outrage in Israel by lying with Jacob's daughter, for such a thing ought not to be done. (NRS)

- **Genesis 34:25** On the third day, when they were still in pain, two of the sons of Jacob, Simeon and Levi, Dinah's brothers, took their swords and came against the city unawares, and killed all the males. (NRS)

What are the appearances of grief revealed in this narrative? How is grief handled?

❖ **Job 1:16** While he was still speaking, another came and said, "The fire of God fell from heaven and burned up the sheep and the servants, and consumed them; I alone have escaped to tell you." (NRS) **Job 1:18** While he was still speaking, another came and said, "Your sons and daughters were eating and drinking wine in their eldest brother's house, (NRS) **Job 1:19** and suddenly a great wind came across the desert, struck the four corners of the house, and it fell on the young people, and they are dead; I alone have escaped to tell you." (NRS)
What are the appearances of grief revealed in this narrative? How is grief handled?

❖ **Ezekiel 24:16** Mortal, with one blow I am about to take away from you the delight of your eyes; yet you shall not mourn or weep, nor shall your tears run down. (NRS) **Ezekiel 24:17** Sigh, but not aloud; make no mourning for the dead. Bind on your turban, and put your sandals on your feet; do not cover your upper lip or eat the bread of mourners. (NRS)

How is Ezekiel told to deal with grief in this narrative? Why would this be a not so positive way to deal with grief?

There are many other biblical narratives that deal with grief (i.e., Proverbs 17, 2 Samuel 19, Luke 15:28, 1 Tim 6:10, 1 Peter 1:6). Each narrative is designed to help us reflect on the message and to change our attitudes and teach practical applications to our lives.

Remember: The scriptures are a resource to help us find meaning to our loss. You do not have to handle grief by yourself. Pastoral Care and other support groups are available to help.

Life Skills Coaching From A Pastoral Care
Perspective
Lesson Two – Depression

Rev. Jamesetta Ferguson - DMin Project
St. Peter's United Church of Christ
July 27, 2011

Introduction

Depression can be defined as a state of sadness, misery, gloominess or unhappiness, accompanied by feelings of hopelessness and inadequacy. In extreme cases depression might be considered a mental disorder resulting in a lack of energy and difficulty in maintaining concentration or interest in life.

The exact cause of depression is not known. Many researchers believe it is caused by chemical changes in the brain. This may be due to a problem with your genes, or triggered by certain stressful events. More likely, it's a combination of both. It's natural to feel down sometimes, but if that low mood lingers day after day, it could signal depression. Major depression is an episode of sadness or apathy along with other symptoms that lasts at least two consecutive weeks and is severe enough to interrupt daily activities. Depression is not a sign of weakness or a negative personality. It is a major public health problem and a treatable medical condition. [78]

Some types of depression run in families. But depression can also occur if you have no family history of the illness. Anyone can develop depression, even kids. The following may play a role in depression

- Alcohol or drug abuse
- Certain medical conditions, including underactive thyroid, cancer, or long-term pain
- Certain medications such as steroids
- Sleeping problems
- Stressful life events, such as:
  - Breaking up with a boyfriend or girlfriend
  - Failing a class
  - Death or illness of someone close to you
  - Divorce
  - Childhood abuse or neglect
  - Job loss
  - Social isolation (common in the elderly)

<u>Symptoms</u>

Depression can change or distort the way you see yourself, your life, and those around you. People who have depression usually see everything with a more negative attitude, unable to imagine that any problem or situation can be solved in a positive way.

Symptoms of depression can include:
- Agitation, restlessness, and irritability
- Dramatic change in appetite, often with weight gain or loss
- Very difficult to concentrate
- Fatigue and lack of energy
- Feelings of hopelessness and helplessness
- Feelings of worthlessness, self-hate, and guilt
- Becoming withdrawn or isolated
- Loss of interest or pleasure in activities that were once enjoyed
- Thoughts of death or suicide
- Trouble sleeping or excessive sleeping

Depression can appear as anger and discouragement, rather than feelings of sadness. If depression is very severe, there may also be psychotic symptoms, such as hallucinations and delusions. [79]

Depression in the Scriptures

Let us take a look at two instances in which the bible discusses depression. Psalm 55:2, 4-8

> *² Please listen and answer me, for I am overwhelmed by my troubles. ⁴ My heart pounds in my chest. The terror of death assaults me. ⁵ Fear and trembling overwhelm me, and I can't stop shaking. ⁶ Oh that I had wings like a dove; then I would fly away and rest! ⁷ I would fly far away to the quiet of the wilderness. ⁸ How quickly I would escape—far from this wild storm of hatred.*

King David had various times of normal depression. Through his journey in life there were periods that he just didn't know what to do; yet he remained connected to God.

Depression as a result of sin is narrated in the book of Jonah 1-4. Jonah became so distraught that he asked God to take his life Jonah 4:3 There are several examples of situational depression in the book of Jonah.[80]

There are many other biblical narratives that deal with depression. Genesis 4:6-7, Psalm 13:2 ; Psalm 16:8,

Psalm 32:3-5, Psalm 88:1-5 and Matthew 26:38 are just a few. There are also many scriptures to deal with <u>hope</u> for those suffering with depression. A few of my favorites are Job 23:10, Proverbs 3:5-6, Matthew 11:28, 1 John 1:9, James 1:12, Philippians' 4:6-7. Others are 2 Corinthians 1:3-4, Ephesians 1:17-19, Hebrews 12:2.

Each narrative is designed to help us reflect on the message and to change our attitudes and teach practical applications to our lives.

<u>Remember:</u> <u>You do not have to handle depression by yourself. Pastoral Care and other support groups are available to help.</u> If you have thoughts of suicide or harming yourself or others, immediately call your local emergency number (such as 911) or go to the hospital emergency room. You may also call a suicide hotline from anywhere in the United States, 24 hours a day, and 7 days a week: 1-800-SUICIDE or 1-800-999-9999.

Call your doctor right away if:

- You hear voices that are not there.
- You have frequent crying spells with little or no reason.
- Your depression is disrupting work, school, or family life.
- You think that your current medications are not working or are causing side effects. Never change or stop any medications without consulting your doctor.

Do not drink alcohol or use illegal drugs. These substances can make depression worse and might lead to thoughts of suicide.

Take your medication exactly as your doctor instructed. Ask your doctor about the possible side effects and what you should do if you have any. Learn to recognize the early signs that your depression is getting worse.

The following tips might help you feel better:

- Get more exercise
- Maintain good sleep habits
- Seek out activities that bring you pleasure
- Volunteer or get involved in group activities
- Talk to someone you trust about how you are feeling
- Try to be around people who are caring and positive

Life Skills Coaching From A Pastoral Care Prospective

Lesson Three – Anger

Rev. Jamesetta Ferguson - DMin Project
St. Peter's United Church of Christ
August 3, 2011

Introduction

Anger can be defined as a powerful emotion. It can be positive or negative anger can be considered healthy such as a survival tool or source of energy, for instance the anxiety we feel from anger might be a warning or signal of danger; signaling us to fight or flee. But anger can also be un-healthy; when it becomes long-drawn out or repressed.

The feeling of anger can be a response to pain, both physical and psychological; and can even be considered a secondary emotion. A primary feeling is what we feel before we get angry. We might first feel afraid, attacked, offended, disrespected, forced, trapped, or pressured. Our response to the primary feeling often is the emotion of anger.

Symptoms: [81]

- Head, stomach and back aches
- Rapid speech
- Yelling and screaming
- Sarcasm or cynicism
- Denial or rationalization about your behavior
- Revenge fantasies
- Thoughts about drinking or using drugs
- Arguing with others
- Becoming silent or withholding
- Avoiding Others
- Isolation
- Becoming Violent
- Compulsive eating, spending, cleaning, or sex

Anger in the Scriptures

Genesis 4:4-7 (NLT) [4] Abel also brought a gift—the best of the firstborn lambs from his flock. The LORD accepted Abel and his gift, [5] but he did not accept Cain and his gift. This made Cain very angry, and he looked dejected. [6] "Why are you so angry?" the LORD asked Cain. "Why do you look so dejected? [7] You will be accepted if you do what is right. But if you refuse to do what is right, then watch out! Sin is crouching at the door, eager to control you. But you must subdue it and be its master."

1 Samuel 18:7-9 (NLT) ⁷ This was their song: "Saul has killed his thousands, and David his ten thousands!" ⁸ This made Saul very angry. "What's this?" he said. "They credit David with ten thousands and me with only thousands. Next they'll be making him their king!" ⁹ So from that time on Saul kept a jealous eye on David.

Psalm 37:7-9 (NLT) 7 Be still in the presence of the LORD, and wait patiently for him to act. Don't worry about evil people who prosper or fret about their wicked schemes. ⁸ Stop being angry! Turn from your rage! Do not lose your temper—it only leads to harm. ⁹ For the wicked will be destroyed, but those who trust in the LORD will possess the land.

Proverbs 29:21-23 (NLT) 21 A servant pampered from childhood will become a rebel. ²² An angry person starts fights; a hot-tempered person commits all kinds of sin. ²³ Pride ends in humiliation, while humility brings honor.

Ecclesiastes 5:16-18 (NLT) 16 And this, too, is a very serious problem. People leave this world no better off than when they came. All their hard work is for nothing—like working for the wind. ¹⁷ Throughout their lives, they live under a cloud—frustrated, discouraged, and angry.

Isaiah 57:16-18 (NLT) ¹⁶ For I will not fight against you forever; I will not always be angry. If I were, all people would pass away—all the souls I have made. ¹⁷ I was angry, so I punished these greedy people. I withdrew from them, but they kept going on their own stubborn way.

Matthew 5:21-26 (NLT) 21 "You have heard that our ancestors were told, 'You must not murder. If you commit murder, you are subject to judgment.' 22 But I say, if you are even angry with someone, you are subject to judgment! If you call someone an idiot, you are in danger of being brought before the court. And if you curse someone, you are in danger of the fires of hell.23 "So if you are presenting a sacrifice at the altar in the Temple and you suddenly remember that someone has something against you, 24 leave your sacrifice there at the altar. Go and be reconciled to that person. Then come and offer your sacrifice to God. 25 "When you are on the way to court with your adversary, settle your differences quickly. Otherwise, your accuser may hand you over to the judge, who will hand you over to an officer, and you will be thrown into prison. 26 And if that happens, you surely won't be free again until you have paid the last penny.

Mark 10:13-15 (NLT) 13 One day some parents brought their children to Jesus so he could touch and bless them. But the disciples scolded the parents for bothering him. 14 When Jesus saw what was happening, he was angry with his disciples. He said to them, "Let the children come to me. Don't stop them! For the Kingdom of God belongs to those who are like these children. 15 I tell you the truth, anyone who doesn't receive the Kingdom of God like a child will never enter it."

Ephesians 4: 26-32 (NLT) 26And "don't sin by letting anger control you." Don't let the sun go down while you are still angry, 27 for anger gives a foothold to the devil. 28 If you are a thief, quit stealing. Instead, use your hands for good hard work, and then give generously to others in need.

²⁹ Don't use foul or abusive language. Let everything you say be good and helpful, so that your words will be an encouragement to those who hear them. ³⁰ And do not bring sorrow to God's Holy Spirit by the way you live. Remember, he has identified you as his own, guaranteeing that you will be saved on the day of redemption. ³¹ Get rid of all bitterness, rage, anger, harsh words, and slander, as well as all types of evil behavior. ³² Instead, be kind to each other, tenderhearted, forgiving one another, just as God through Christ has forgiven you.

James 1:19 (NLT) 19 Understand this, my dear brothers and sisters: You must all be quick to listen, slow to speak, and slow to get angry.

Biblical Principal to break the stronghold of anger (2 Corinthians 10:3-7 (NLT)

2 Corinthians 10:3-7 ³ We are human, but we don't wage war as humans do. ⁴We use God's mighty weapons, not worldly weapons, to knock down the strongholds of human reasoning and to destroy false arguments. ⁵ We destroy every proud obstacle that keeps people from knowing God. We capture their rebellious thoughts and teach them to obey Christ. ⁶ And after you have become fully obedient, we will punish everyone who remains disobedient. ⁷ Look at the obvious facts. Those who say they belong to Christ must recognize that we belong to Christ as much as they do.

Biblical Principal to face the real issues (Gal 5:13-26) (NLT)

Galatians 5:13-26 (NLT) 13 For you have been called to live in freedom, my brothers and sisters. But don't use your freedom to satisfy your sinful nature. Instead, use your freedom to serve one another in love. ¹⁴ For the whole law can be summed up in this one command: "Love your neighbor as yourself." ¹⁵ But if you are always biting and devouring one another, watch out! Beware of destroying one another. ¹⁶ So I say, let the Holy Spirit guide your lives. Then you won't be doing what your sinful nature craves. ¹⁷ The sinful nature wants to do evil, which is just the opposite of what the Spirit wants. And the Spirit gives us desires that are the opposite of what the sinful nature desires. These two forces are constantly fighting each other, so you are not free to carry out your good intentions. ¹⁸ But when you are directed by the Spirit, you are not under obligation to the Law of Moses. ¹⁹ When you follow the desires of your sinful nature, the results are very clear: sexual immorality, impurity, lustful pleasures, ²⁰ idolatry, sorcery, hostility, quarreling, jealousy, outbursts of anger, selfish ambition, dissension, division, ²¹ envy, drunkenness, wild parties, and other sins like these. Let me tell you again, as I have before, that anyone living that sort of life will not inherit the Kingdom of God. ²² But the Holy Spirit produces this kind of fruit in our lives: love, joy, peace, patience, kindness, goodness, faithfulness, ²³ gentleness, and self-control. There is no law against these things! ²⁴ Those who belong to Christ Jesus have nailed the passions and desires of their sinful nature to his cross and crucified them there. ²⁵ Since we are living by the Spirit, let us follow the Spirit's leading in every part of our lives. ²⁶ Let us not become conceited, or provoke one another, or be jealous of one another.

Remember: You do not have to handle anger by yourself.

Pastoral Care and other support groups are available to help.

Life Skills Coaching From A Pastoral Care Prospective

Lesson Four – Fear

Rev. Jamesetta Ferguson - DMin Project
St. Peter's United Church of Christ
Aug 10, 2011

Fear

Introduction

In the past three lessons we have discussed emotions normally categorized as secondary emotions; grief, depression and anger. Secondary emotions appear as a result of the primary emotions or they may be caused directly by them. For example where the fear of a threat turns to anger that may trigger the body to prepare to fight.

Fear, our lesson for today, is considered a primary emotion. As previously discussed, primary emotions are those that we feel first, as an initial response to a situation. Thus, if we are threatened, we may feel fear. When we hear of a death, we may feel sadness. The emotion of fear is unthinking, natural responses that we have. We even see it revealed in how animals react in situations.

Typical primary emotions include fear, anger, sadness and happiness (sometimes these can also be felt as secondary emotions). It's important for us to remember that fear happens to all of us. Fear can range from a little scare to paralyzing terror.

As humans, our need for controlling things and situations in our lives and around us is, to some extent, fear-driven. If I cannot control the world around me, it may threaten me. My anticipation of future events is enough to cause me to fear.

Pessimism (i.e., cup half empty instead of half full) can lead to fear, as we habitually predict that we will fail or that bad things will happen to us. Because we can never fully anticipate the future, we may live in a permanent state of fear.

Much has been made of the fear of death, which we know we will all ultimately face. Terrorists are trained to believe that their death may be worthy of the cause, and because of this they do not fear the outcome.

Fear can also happen from confusion, which happens when we are unable to gather meaning. The logic of this goes something like 'I can't find any meaning. I don't know if it will harm me. I'd better feel frightened, just in case.'

When people recognize something fearful a common response is to get away from it somehow. If, however, the subject of fear is vague and there is no clear escape, then a common alternative response is to deny the fear, pretending that it does not exist.

Symptoms
- Mild or extreme muscular tension (danger)
- Fainting (shocking incident)
- Adrenalin rush (roller coaster ride, mountain gliding)
- Losing the content of our bowels
- Phobias (snakes; crowds)

Fear is thus useful when you want to move a person *away* from something. It can also be used to shake them out of their current complacency. Fear is a *push* strategy. It is often best followed up with something that *pulls* the other person towards the desired objective.[82] The fear of incarceration can cause a person to admit a drug or alcohol problem, seeking the help they need to live their life differently.

At the age of 45 God called me to go to the seminary. I had been in church all my life, however, at the seminary I was asked to take different classes and to expand my understanding of who God is in the world. There was a lot of fear and anxiety on my part as to whether I could succeed in school again. I had a friend and sister remind me that if God brought me to it, God will bring me through it. Reminding me that when I rely on God as my source and strength, that even in the midst of fear, faith will challenge me to confront the fear and try it anyway.

Now let us review several biblical passages that address fear.

Fear in the Scriptures

1. **God is the answer to a fearful heart.**
   Psalm 34:4 - I prayed to the LORD, and he answered me. He freed me from all my fears.
   1 Peter 5:7 - Give all your worries and cares to God, for he cares about you.
2. **Focus not on fear but on what is real and true.**
   Psalm 4:8 In peace I will lie down and sleep, for you alone, O LORD, will keep me safe.
   Philippians 4:8- And now, dear brothers and sisters, one final thing. Fix your thoughts on what is true, and honorable, and right, and pure, and lovely, and admirable. Think about things that are excellent and worthy of praise.

   Philippians 4:13- For I can do everything through Christ, who gives me strength.

3. God is present with us in every situation.
Deuteronomy 31:8 - Do not be afraid or discouraged, for the LORD will personally go ahead of you. He will be with you; he will neither fail you nor abandon you.

Isaiah 41:10 - Don't be afraid, for I am with you. Don't be discouraged, for I am your God. I will strengthen you and help you. I will hold you up with my victorious right hand.

4. We must not fear the past or the future.
Isaiah 43:18-19 - [18] "But forget all that—it is nothing compared to what I am going to do. [19] For I am about to do something new. See, I have already begun! Do you not see it? I will make a pathway through the wilderness. I will create rivers in the dry wasteland.

Philippians 3:13-14 - [13] No, dear brothers and sisters, I have not achieved it,[a] but I focus on this one thing: Forgetting the past and looking forward to what lies ahead, [14] I press on to reach the end of the race and receive the heavenly prize for which God, through Christ Jesus, is calling us.

<u>**Remember:** You do not have to handle Fear by yourself. Pastoral Care and other support groups are available to help.</u>
**Pastoral Care – Rev. Jamesetta Ferguson, Senior Pastor St. Peter's United Church of Christ – (502) 583-5544
(502) 417-8438 cell

Life Skills Coaching From A Pastoral Care Prospective

Lesson Five – Positive Relationships

Rev. Jamesetta Ferguson - DMin Project
St. Peter's United Church of Christ
Aug 17, 2011

Introduction
Good interaction with family, friends, co-workers and the people we are around is necessary for living in a healthy community. No person is an island, meaning we share our lives with other human beings in all functions or life, and we must be able to deal with others in a respectful and caring way.

One of the goals of St. Peter's is to provide a positive environment in which persons are prepared to live, work and enjoy a healthy life with their community. Another description for this is positive relationships.

The initial development stage of building a positive relationship is trust. We have built a trust within this small group over the past five weeks through the establishment of appropriate personal boundaries for interaction, open communication and the creation of a safe environment for cultural differences and diversity. These are three important factors that I believe are key to developing healthy relationships including family, friend, co-workers and the community in which we live.

Webster's Dictionary defines trust as assured reliance on the character, ability, strength, or truth of someone or something, or one in which confidence is placed.[83] Children have a natural instinct to trust their parents or the adults that raise them, believing that they will provide their physical, emotional and social needs. Many times when people have been physically, sexually, or emotionally abused as children they lose their ability to determine whom they can trust.

When individuals commit to marriage with one another; with confidence they believe that their partner will be honest, faithful and committed to the marriage. However, when the partner has an affair with another individual or hides other secrets that causes mistrust within the relationship.

When people deposit money in the bank; believing that when they go to get money out of the bank it will be there to withdraw that is a trusting relationship. Yet, some people hide their money under mattresses or other places within their homes because they do not believe their money is safe unless they see it for themselves. They mistrust and lack confidence in the institution.

Additional factors that help build trust is the establishment of appropriate personal boundaries. This can be defined as rules or limits that each of us creates to identify who we are and the behavior or expectation we will allow from the people around. It also helps determine our response when someone steps outside those limits. Personal boundaries help with our self-esteem and opinion of our self-worth. Setting boundaries involves learning to love and respect ourselves, and our time and resources.

Boundaries have been established for these life skills lessons to honor one another by keeping the discussion contained with the individual sessions, by letting you know that each person has a choice to participate in discussion and will not be ridiculed for not participating. Disparaging or disrespectful remarks are not allowed. Finally there has been an intentional effort to demonstrate love, respect, and honesty toward each other, modeling those same virtues and qualities which Christ shows us.

Open communication goes beyond simply voicing our opinion, but also includes active listening. In other words there are times that we need to stop talking and let others talk as we listen. Effective communication is the key to getting you to where you want to be in your life and is an essential skill for successful relationships of any kind. Listening makes the person we are communicating with feel worthy, appreciated, interesting, and respected.

In our family relationships, greater communication brings greater intimacy. When parents listen to their children it helps build their self-esteem. In community, listening helps prevent misunderstandings between people with whom we casually interact and can foster learning. Communication has the power to destroy, or build relationships.[84]

Finally, the creation of a safe environment for cultural differences and diversity promotes trust and encourages a positive relationship. The United States is a highly diverse nation racially and culturally, yet we all share this country together. Positive relationships recognize our differences and have a healthy respect for our brothers and sisters understanding that we are individuals, all made in the image of God. God made us different from one another and there is no mistake. What would your actions reveal as the answer to these questions? I'm aware of the differences in personality, values, interests, and cultures of different people, and I adapt the way I relate to them accordingly. I like to be helpful and supportive of others, and consider their interests and needs as well as my own.

Positive Relationships in the Scriptures

Positive interaction with people goes far beyond simply being near them and speaking with them. That can be difficult in any group of people including the church. However, the scriptures as taught by Jesus, give us a guide to use in interacting positively with our brothers and sisters as we journey through life.

Luke 10:27-37 (NLT) 27 The man answered, "'You must love the LORD your God with all your heart, all your soul, all your strength, and all your mind.' And, 'Love your neighbor as yourself.'" 28 "Right!" Jesus told him. "Do this and you will live!" 29 The man wanted to justify his actions, so he asked Jesus, "And who is my neighbor?"

The Good Samaritan

30 Jesus replied with a story: "A Jewish man was traveling on a trip from Jerusalem to Jericho, and he was attacked by bandits. They stripped him of his clothes, beat him up, and left him half dead beside the road. 31 "By chance a priest came along. But when he saw the man lying there, he

crossed to the other side of the road and passed him by. ³² A Temple assistant walked over and looked at him lying there, but he also passed by on the other side. ³³ "Then a despised Samaritan came along, and when he saw the man, he felt compassion for him. ³⁴ Going over to him, the Samaritan soothed his wounds with olive oil and wine and bandaged them. Then he put the man on his own donkey and took him to an inn, where he took care of him. ³⁵ The next day he handed the innkeeper two silver coins telling him, 'Take care of this man. If his bill runs higher than this, I'll pay you the next time I'm here.' ³⁶ "Now which of these three would you say was a neighbor to the man who was attacked by bandits?" Jesus asked. ³⁷ The man replied, "The one who showed him mercy."
Then Jesus said, "Yes, now go and do the same."

Proverbs 16:7 *(NLT) 7 When people's lives please the* LORD, *even their enemies are at peace with them.*

Luke 6:27-45 (NLT)
Love for Enemies
²⁷ *"But to you who are willing to listen, I say, love your enemies! Do good to those who hate you. ²⁸ Bless those who curse you. Pray for those who hurt you. ²⁹ If someone slaps you on one cheek, offer the other cheek also. If someone demands your coat, offer your shirt also. ³⁰ Give to anyone who asks; and when things are taken away from you, don't try to get them back. ³¹ Do to others as you would like them to do to you. ³² "If you love only those who love you, why should you get credit for that? Even sinners love those who love them! ³³ And if you do good only to those who do good to you, why should you get credit? Even sinners do that much! ³⁴ And if you lend*

money only to those who can repay you, why should you get credit? Even sinners will lend to other sinners for a full return. ³⁵ *"Love your enemies! Do good to them. Lend to them without expecting to be repaid. Then your reward from heaven will be very great, and you will truly be acting as children of the Most High, for he is kind to those who are unthankful and wicked.* ³⁶ *You must be compassionate, just as your Father is compassionate.*

Do Not Judge Others
³⁷ *"Do not judge others, and you will not be judged. Do not condemn others, or it will all come back against you. Forgive others, and you will be forgiven.* ³⁸ *Give, and you will receive. Your gift will return to you in full—pressed down, shaken together to make room for more, running over, and poured into your lap. The amount you give will determine the amount you get back."* ³⁹ *Then Jesus gave the following illustration: "Can one blind person lead another? Won't they both fall into a ditch?* ⁴⁰ *Students are not greater than their teacher. But the student who is fully trained will become like the teacher.* ⁴¹ *"And why worry about a speck in your friend's eye when you have a log in your own?* ⁴² *How can you think of saying, 'Friend, let me help you get rid of that speck in your eye,' when you can't see past the log in your own eye? Hypocrite! First get rid of the log in your own eye; then you will see well enough to deal with the speck in your friend's eye.*

The Tree and It's Fruit
⁴³ *"A good tree can't produce bad fruit, and a bad tree can't produce good fruit.* ⁴⁴ *A tree is identified by its fruit. Figs are never gathered from thorn bushes, and grapes are not picked from bramble bushes.* ⁴⁵ *A good person produces good things from the treasury of a good heart, and an evil*

person produces evil things from the treasury of an evil heart. What you say flows from what is in your heart.

Remember: Pastoral Care and other support groups are available to help if you are interested in fostering positive relationships.

**Pastoral Care – Rev. Jamesetta Ferguson, Senior Pastor
St. Peter's United Church of Christ – (502) 583-5544
(502) 417-8438 cell

Life Skills Coaching From A Pastoral Care Perspective

Lesson Six – Healthy Marriage

Rev. Jamesetta Ferguson - DMin Project
St. Peter's United Church of Christ
Aug 24, 2011

Healthy Marriage
Introduction
Last week we discussed various key elements in building healthy relationships. Again the initial development stage of building a positive relationship is trust. Webster's Dictionary defines trust as assured reliance on the character, ability, strength, or truth of someone or something, or one in which confidence is placed[85] Trust is built through the establishment of appropriate personal boundaries for interaction, open communication and the creation of a safe environment for cultural differences and diversity. Healthy marriages are based on positive relationships; therefore the ingredients are the same.

In this day and time when marriage is not promoted or encouraged, marriage remains the desire of God for all of us at some point in our lives. Healthy marriages in many instances include praying together, making important decisions together, attending church together and continue dating one another.

Healthy Marriages in the Scriptures

Falling in love may have seemed effortless, but keeping your marriage strong will take ongoing work. Building a healthy marriage is not all that complicated or difficult if you're determined to follow a few basic principles.

Marriage is part of God's design for us.

Genesis 2:22-25 [22] Then the LORD God made a woman from the rib, and he brought her to the man. [23] "At last!" the man exclaimed. "This one is bone from my bone, and flesh from my flesh! She will be called 'woman,' because she was taken from 'man.' [24] This explains why a man leaves his father and mother and is joined to his wife, and the two are united into one. [25] Now the man and his wife were both naked, but they felt no shame.

Marriage is a covenant

Malachi 2:14 You cry out, "Why doesn't the LORD accept my worship?" I'll tell you why! Because the LORD witnessed the vows you and your wife made when you were young. But you have been unfaithful to her, though she remained your faithful partner, the wife of your marriage vows.

Hebrew 13:4 Give honor to marriage, and remain faithful to one another in marriage. God will surely judge people who are immoral and those who commit adultery.

1 Corinthians 7:2 But because there is so much sexual immorality, each man should have his own wife, and each woman should have her own husband.

Should you marry an unbeliever?

2 Corinthians 6:14 [14] Don't team up with those who are unbelievers. How can righteousness be a partner with wickedness? How can light live with darkness?

Role in Marriage

Husband

Ephesians 5:23-28 [23] A husband is the head of his wife, as Christ is the head and the Savior of the church, which is his own body. [24] Wives should always put their husbands first, as the church puts Christ first.

[25] A husband should love his wife as much as Christ loved the church and gave his life for it. [26] He made the church holy by the power of his word, and he made it pure by washing it with water. [27] Christ did this, so that he would have a glorious and holy church, without faults or spots or wrinkles or any other flaws.

[28] In the same way, a husband should love his wife as much as he loves himself. A husband who loves his wife shows that he loves himself.

1 Peter 3:7 In the same way, you husbands must give honor to your wives. Treat your wife with understanding as you live together. She may be weaker than you are, but she is your equal partner in God's gift of new life. Treat her as you should so your prayers will not be hindered.

Colossians 3:19 A husband must love his wife and not abuse her.

Wife
Genesis 2:18 The LORD God said, "It isn't good for the man to live alone. I need to make a suitable partner for him."

Ephesians 5:22-23 [22] A wife should put her husband first, as she does the Lord. [23] A husband is the head of his wife, as Christ is the head and the Savior of the church, which is his own body.

Proverbs 14:1 A woman's family is held together by her wisdom, but it can be destroyed by her foolishness.
Proverbs 19:13-14 [13] A foolish son brings disgrace to his father. A nagging wife goes on and on like the drip, drip, drip of the rain. [14] You may inherit all you own from your parents, but a sensible wife is a gift from the LORD.

1 Peter 3:1 If you are a wife, you must put your husband first. Even if he opposes our message, you will win him over by what you do. No one else will have to say anything to him.

Remember: Pastoral Care and other support groups are available for marriage support.

**Pastoral Care – Rev. Jamesetta Ferguson, Senior Pastor St. Peter's United Church of Christ – (502) 583-5544 (502) 417-8438 cell

Life Skills Coaching From A Pastoral Care Perspective

Lesson Seven – Parenting

Rev. Jamesetta Ferguson - DMin Project
St. Peter's United Church of Christ
Aug 31, 2011

Parenting
Introduction
Parenting is a skill and it's a hard one to learn at that. Being a parent is a joyous thing, but good parenting skills are something that you have to continuously work at. You will never be a "perfect" parent, because we all mistakes. Here are a few tips to ensure that you are being the best parent that you can be.

1. Show Love
Always give your children a lot of love. Tell them "I love you" and make sure they know that they are special to you. Provide them with a lot of hugs and kisses and always be there when they need a shoulder to cry on.

2. Listen When Your Child Talks
Listening to your children really stresses to them that they are important. No matter how strange or ridiculous it may be, listen to your child's stories, ideas and complaints. When you listen to your children then they know that you

are interested in what they have to say. Don't just pretend to be listening, as children can quickly see that you are really not that interested and that you are just pretending.

3. Make Your Child Feel Safe
Children are defenseless in life and things they don't understand or are scary to them may easily scare them. Comforting your child at every stage in life will provide them with the security they need. They need to know that you are there for them and that you will protect them. They also need to see that you have taken steps to protect them.

4. Provide Order and Organization
Children need a regular daily schedule. They need to have meals, naps and bedtimes at consistent times throughout the day. When they come home they need to do their homework and their chores before they can play. Before they go to bed they need to take a bath, brush their teeth and get their school supplies ready first. When they get up in the morning they need to eat breakfast, get dressed, brush their teeth, get their belongings together and then they can use any extra time they have for television or a game.

5. Praise Your child
Praise them while they are small. Praise is very important for children to develop and have great self-esteem. They need to know that they are doing well and that you are proud of them. Use frequent pats on the back, smiles and

thumbs up when you see them doing what they are supposed to be doing or when they are doing something well. Too much praise can quickly appear to be fake praise and your children will not appreciate it as much.

6. Criticize Bad Behavior
You don't need to tell your child, "You were bad." In most cases they already know this and they probably knew it when they did whatever it was that they did. Instead, explain what the child did that was wrong. Explain to them what they should have done instead.

7. Consistency is Key
Your rules don't have to be the same rules you had when you were growing up, but whatever rules you choose to have need to be enforced on a consistent basis. This goes for mom and dad, family members and baby sitters. If two parents are raising the child, then they both need to have the same rules.

8. Spend Time with Your Children
Children thrive on the time they get to spend with their parents. Little trips to the park to play with the dog or reading before bedtime will go a long way with your children. Many bad behaviors stem from a lack of attention on the parents part and the child is simply trying to get your attention. [86]

Parenting in the Scriptures

Proverbs 22:6 (NLT)
Start **child**ren off on the way they should go, and even when they are **old** they will not turn from it.

2 Samuel 13 (NLT) [1] In the course of time, Amnon son of David fell in love with Tamar, the beautiful sister of Absalom son of David. [2] Amnon became so obsessed with his sister Tamar that he made himself ill. She was a virgin, and it seemed impossible for him to do anything to her. [3] Now Amnon had an adviser named Jonadab son of Shimeah, David's brother. Jonadab was a very shrewd man. [4] He asked Amnon, "Why do you, the king's son, look so haggard morning after morning? Won't you tell me?" Amnon said to him, "I'm in love with Tamar, my brother Absalom's sister." [5] "Go to bed and pretend to be ill," Jonadab said. "When your father comes to see you, say to him, 'I would like my sister Tamar to come and give me something to eat. Let her prepare the food in my sight so I may watch her and then eat it from her hand.'" [6] So Amnon lay down and pretended to be ill. When the king came to see him, Amnon said to him, "I would like my sister Tamar to come and make some special bread in my sight, so I may eat from her hand." [7] David sent word to Tamar at the palace: "Go to the house of your brother Amnon and prepare some food for him." [8] So Tamar went to the house of her brother Amnon, who was lying down. She took some dough, kneaded it, made the bread in his sight and baked it. [9] Then she took the pan and served him the bread, but he refused to eat. "Send everyone out of here," Amnon said. So everyone left him. [10] Then Amnon said to Tamar, "Bring the food here into my bedroom so I may eat from your hand." And Tamar took the bread she had prepared and brought it to her brother Amnon in his bedroom. ¹¹ But when she took it to him to eat, he grabbed her and said, "Come to bed with me, my sister." ¹² "No, my brother!" she said to him. "Don't force me! Such a thing should not be done in Israel! Don't do this wicked thing. ¹³ What about me? Where could I get rid of my disgrace? And what about you? You would be like one of the wicked fools in Israel. Please speak to the king; he will not keep me from being married to you." ¹⁴ But he refused to listen to her, and since he was stronger than she, he raped her. ¹⁵ Then Amnon hated her with intense hatred. In fact, he hated her more than he had loved her. Amnon said to her, "Get up and get out!" ¹⁶ "No!" she said to him. "Sending me away would be a greater wrong than what you have already done to me." But he refused to listen to her. ¹⁷ He called his personal servant and said, "Get this woman out of my sight and bolt the door after her." ¹⁸ So his servant put her out and bolted the door after her. She was wearing an ornate[a] robe, for this was the kind of garment the virgin daughters of the king wore. ¹⁹ Tamar put ashes on her head and tore the ornate robe she was wearing. She put her hands on her head and went away, weeping aloud as she went. ²⁰ Her brother Absalom said to her, "Has that Amnon, your brother, been with you? Be quiet for now, my sister; he is your brother. Don't take this thing to heart." And Tamar lived in her brother Absalom's house, a desolate woman. ²¹ When King David heard all this, he was furious. ²² And Absalom never said a word to Amnon, either good or bad; he hated Amnon because he had disgraced his sister Tamar.

2 Kings 22:1, 23:25 (NLT) Josiah was eight years old when he became king, and he reigned in Jerusalem thirty-one years. 23:25 Never before had there been a king like **Josiah**, who turned to the Lord with all his heart and soul and strength, obeying all the laws of Moses. And there has never been a king like him since.
Ephesians 6:4 (NLT) 4 Fathers, do not provoke your children to anger by the way you treat them. Rather, bring them up with the discipline and instruction that comes from the Lord.
****

What do you think of this passage?
Hosea 2:4(NLT) And I will not love her children, for they were conceived in prostitution.

Remember: Pastoral Care and other support groups are available for parenting.
**Pastoral Care – Rev. Jamesetta Ferguson, Senior Pastor St. Peter's United Church of Christ – (502) 583-5544 (502) 417-8438 cell

Case Studies for Parenting

1. You come home from work and discover your twelve year old child passed out from obvious drug/alcohol use. What would you do? How would you approach the issue with your child?

2. Your fourteen year old daughter just informed you she was pregnant. What would you do? How would you approach the issue with your child?

3. Your son comes home from school and tells you to get him some condoms because he wants to start having sex. What would you do? How would you approach the issue with your child?

4. You tell your children that you and your wife have decided to end their marriage and are getting a divorce. How would you approach the issue with your children?

5. Your child received a college scholarship and is anxious to tell you about it, but you are busy job hunting and preoccupied with other matters. What do you do?

6. Your child's best friend was shot in a drive by, and he/she witnessed the shooting. What would you do? How would you approach the issue with your child?

7. Your child seems to be out of touch these days. He/she stays in their room and seems to not care. He/she has even started giving away their personal items. What would you do? How would you approach the issue with your child?

8. Your son comes home and tells you he wants to be a dancer instead of playing football. How would you react? How would you approach the issue with your child?

9. Since you and your wife broke up your daughter has been living with you. Now she tells you she wants to go live with Mom. What would you do? How would you approach the issue with your child?

10. You have never seen your child because of being locked up in prison and now the day to finally meet him/her is here. How would you handle this first visit? What would you say to him/her?

APPENDIX E

St. Peter's UCC Life Skills Course
<u>Life Skills Coaching Evaluation Form</u>

1. What is your name?
   _____

2. Please rate the usefulness of the material.

   1 2 3 4 5 6 7 8 9 10 (1 bad....10 good)

3. Please rate the presentation of the material.

   1 2 3 4 5 6 7 8 9 10 (1 bad....10 good)

4. What are five things you learned about life skills that you find useful?

   1. _____
   2. _____
   3. _____
   4. _____
   5. _____

6. Do you feel the information should be an ongoing resource for the church?   Yes   No

7. What is your overall rating of the seven lessons?

    1 2 3 4 5 6 7 8 9 10 (1 bad....10 good)

8. Are there any changes you would like to see in the lesson plan (please write comments on back).

Endnotes

[1] Violet Law, "Life after Lockup," NHI: Shelterforce Online, http://www.nhi.org/online/issues/139/afterlockup.html (accessed March 25, 2013).

[2] Homer U. Ashby, *Our Home Is Over Jordan: a Black Pastoral Theology* (St. Louis, MO: Chalice Press, 2003), 95.

[3] W. J. Wilson, *The Truly Disadvantaged: The Inner City, the Underclass, and Public Policy* (Chicago and London: The University of Chicago Press, 1987), 38.

[4] Dionne J. Jones and Stanley F. Battle, *Teenage pregnancy: developing strategies for change in the twenty-first century* (New Brunswick: Transaction, 1999), 143.

[5] Anne Marshal, "The Truth About Consequences," *Leo Weekly*, February 22, 2012.

[6] U.S. Census Bureau, Census 2000, Summary File 3 (Kentucky State Data Center, 2000) http://www.census.gov/ (accessed January 3, 2012)

[7] Donatelli, Elizabeth, "Hundreds of inmates released early across Kentucky" (January 3, 2012) http://www.wave3.com/ (accessed January 3, 2012).

[8] Alcohol and Public Health, Center for Disease Control and Prevention (Washington, DC, 2012) http://www.cdc.gov/alcohol/faqs.htm/ (accessed July 15, 2012).

[9] 2013 Feeding America, "Solid Foundation for Families, " Advocating Against Hunger. http://feedingamerica.org/how-we-fight-hunger/advocacy-public-policy/solid-foundation-for-families.aspx (accessed February 1, 2013).

¹⁰ Howard Thurman, *Jesus and the Disinherited* (Boston: Beacon Press, 1976), 89, Kindle e-book.

¹¹ Homer U. Ashby, *Our Home Is Over Jordan: a Black Pastoral Theology* (St. Louis, MO: Chalice Press, 2003), 96.

¹² Stacey Floyd-Thomas et al., *Black Church Studies: An Introduction* (Nashville, TN: Abingdon Press, 2007), 123, Kindle e-book.

¹³ Michelle Alexander, *The New Jim Crow: Mass Incarceration in the Age of Colorblindness* (New York: The New Press, 2010, 2012), 187, Kindle e-book.

¹⁴ Pew Center on the States, "Kentucky: A Data-Driven Effort to Protect Public Safety and Control Corrections Spending" (October 2010), http://www.dpa.ky.gov/NR/rdonlyres/1DD65541-F32F-4447-BE51-6D891C20CB6A/0/103_10_PSPPKentuckyBrief_print.pdf (accessed February 11, 2011).

¹⁵ S. C. Andreescu, *Racial Fairness in Sentencing: A Case Study of Selected Crimes in Jefferson County*. Racial Fairness Commission, Commonwealth of Kentucky Court of Justice. (Louisville: Urban Studies Institute, School of Urban and Public Affairs, University of Louisville, 2004), 31.

¹⁶ Pew Center on the States, "Kentucky: A Data-Driven Effort to Protect Public Safety and Control Corrections Spending" (October 2010), http://www.dpa.ky.gov/NR/rdonlyres/1DD65541-F32F-4447-BE51-6D891C20CB6A/0/103_10_PSPPKentuckyBrief_print.pdf (accessed February 11, 2011).

¹⁷United Church of Christ, "Basis of Union, Beliefs," http://www.ucc.org/beliefs/basis-of-union.html (accessed February 2, 2013).

¹⁸ Daniel Johnson et al., eds., *Theology and Identity* (New York: Pilgrim Press, 1990), 31.

[19] United Church of Christ, "UCC Brand Guidelines" About Us, http://www.ucc.org/about-us/ucc-logo.html (accessed February 11, 2013).

[20] N. Hengeveld, ed.,"Matthew 28:18-20 NIV," Bible Gateway, http://www.biblegateway.com/passage/ (accessed February 11, 2013).

[21] Douglas Horton, *The United Church of Christ. Its Origins, Organization, and Role in the World* (New York: Thomas Nelson & Sons, 1962), 67.

[22] Dean Bucalos, *Mission Behind Bars & Beyond*, Missionbehindbarsandbeyond.org, (accessed February 10, 2011).

[23] Dwight N. Hopkins, ed., *Black Faith & Public Talk* (Waco: Baylor University Press, 2007), 79.

[24] G. S.Wilmore, "Black Spiritual Churches," in *African American Religious Studies,* ed. H.A. Baer (Durham and London: Duke University Press,1989), 95.

[25] Rev. Joseph Healey, Moderator, "It takes a whole village to raise a child," African Proverb of the Month, November, 1998, http://www.afriprov.org/ (accessed March 1, 2012).

[26] Gregory Boyle, *Tattoos on the Heart: The Power of Boundless Compassion* (New York: Free Press, 2011), 187, Kindle e-book.

[27] United Church of Christ Justice & Witness Ministries, Wider Church Ministries, *2011-2012 Public Policy Briefing Book* (Cleveland: Pilgrim Press, 2011), 12-14.

[28] Helen Kromer, *Amistad: the Slave Uprising Aboard the Spanish Schooner* (Cleveland, Ohio: Pilgrim Press, 1997), 5.

[29] Justice and Witness Ministries of the United Church of Christ, "Doing Justice: A Bible study and reflection guide" (Cleveland: United Church Press, 2001), 1-12.

[30]UCC Mission Statement on Health and Human Services, General Synod 15, http://www.ucc.org/health/pdfs/ucchealthhumanservice-missionstatement.pdf (accessed November 10, 2012).

[31] Barbara T. Baylor, MPH Minister for Health Care Justice, http://www.ucc.org/justice/health/ (accessed Feb 13, 2013).

[32] Kevin W. Mannoia and Don Thorsen, eds., *The Holiness Manifesto* (Grand Rapids: Wm. B. Eermans Publishers, 2008), 193.

[33]Martin Luther King Multi-Purpose Center, "The Mission," http://www.martinlutherking-mpc.org/home.cfm (accessed March, 2013).

[34] Stacey Floyd-Thomas et al., *Black Church Studies: An Introduction* (Nashville, TN: Abingdon Press, 2007), 140, Kindle e-book.

[35] Clayborne Carson, "Martin Luther King, Jr., and the African-American Social Gospel," in *African American Religious Thought: An Anthology,* ed. Cornell West (Louisville: Westminster John Knox Press, 2003), 704.

[36] Carson, 711.

[37] N. Hengeveld, ed.," Micah 6:7-9, CEV," *Bible Gateway*, http://www.biblegateway.com/ (accessed February 11, 2013)

[38] Howard Thurman, *Deep River: An Interpretation of Negro Spirituals (*Mills College: Eucalyptus Press,1945), 1.

[39] James A. Cone, *Black Theology* Vol. 2. (Maryknoll: Orbis Books, 2003), 38.

[40] Howard Thurman, *Jesus and the Disinherited* (Boston: Beacon Press, 1976), 29, Kindle e-book.

[41] James A. Cone, *Black Theology* Vol. 2. (Maryknoll: Orbis Books, 2003), 199.

[42] Cone, 219.

[43] Will Coleman, *Tribal Talk: Black Theology, Hermeneutics, and African/American Ways of Telling the Story* (University Park: Pennsylvania State University Press, 2000), 180.

[44] James H. Cone, *God of the Oppressed* (Maryknoll: Orbis Books, 1997), 213.

[45] Albert B. Cleage Jr., *Black Christian Nationalism: New Directions for the Black Church* (New York: Luxor Publishers of the Pan-African Orthodox Christian Church, 1987), 31.

[46] James O. Stallings, *Telling the Story: Evangelism in Black Churches* (Valley Forge: Judson Press, 1988), 20.

[47] Stephen G. Ray, *Do No Harm: Social Sin and Christian Responsibility* (Minneapolis: Fortress Press, 2003), 34.

[48] Edward P. Wimberly, *African American Pastoral Care*, rev. ed. (Nashville: Abingdon Press, 2008), 101, Kindle e-book.

[49] James H. Cone, "God and Black Suffering: Calling the Oppressors to Account," *Anglican Theological Review,* 90, no. 4 (2008): 710.

[50] Karen Lebacqz, *Six Theories of Justice* (Minneapolis: Augsburg Publishing House, 1986), 117.

[51] Emilie M. Townes, *Embracing the Spirit: Womanist Perspectives on Hope, Salvation, and Transformation* (Maryknoll: Orbis Books, 1997), 123.

[52] Townes, 122-123.

[53] Ibid., 191.

⁵⁴ Stacey Floyd-Thomas et al., *Black Church Studies: An Introduction* (Nashville, TN: Abingdon Press, 2007), 197, Kindle e-book.

⁵⁵Floyd-Thomas, 124.

⁵⁶ Robert Beckford, *Dread and Pentecostal: a Political Theology for the Black Church in Britain* (Eugene, OR: Wipf & Stock Publishers, 2011), 5.

⁵⁷ Victoria Johnson., CPE Director, Baptist FellowshipCenter, Pastoral Counseling Center, Basic Life Skills DMin Project, Louisville (2010)

⁵⁸ Carl Savage and William Presnell, *Narrative Research in Ministry: a Postmodern Research Approach for Faith Communities* (Louisville: Wayne E. Oates Institute, 2008), 86.

⁵⁹ Daniel Meadows, "What About Digital Storytelling," Educational Uses of Digital Storytelling, http://digitalstorytelling.coe.uh.edu/ (accessed June 9, 2011).

⁶⁰ Jim Watkins, The Christian Broadcasting Network, "Dealing with Grief," http://The Christian Broadcasting Network.com/ (accessed July 16, 2011).

⁶¹June Hunt, *How to Handle Your Emotions: Anger, Depression, Fear, Grief, Rejection, Self-Worth,* Counseling through the Bible Series (Eugene, OR: Harvest House Publishers, 2008), 80-81, Kindle e-book.

⁶² Thomas Hollander, "13 Signs of Anger and How To (Br) Manage Them in Sobriety," *Self Help Magazine*, http://www.selfhelpmagazine.com/article/alchohol-anger/ (accessed August 3, 2011).

⁶³ Khairul Baharein Mohd Noor, "Case Study: A Strategic Research Methodology," *American Journal of Applied Science*, 5(11):1602-1604: 208.

[64] Donald P. Smith, *Empowering Ministry: Ways to Grow in Effectiveness* (Louisville: Westminster John Knox Press, 1996), 69.

[65] The statistical test was prepared by Ashantye Jones, MSSW, MPA, Kent School of Social Work, University of Louisville, KY.

[66] Public Health Ontario Partners for Health, The Health Communication Unit," Summary of Social Sciences," http://www.thcu.ca/ (accessed June 13, 2011).

[67] Christie Cozad Neuger, James Newton Poling, eds., *The Care of Men* (Nashville: Abingdon Press, 1997), 50.

[68] John Dewar Gleissner, *Prison & Slavery - a Surprising Comparison* (Denver: Outskirts Press, 2010), 26, Kindle e-book.

[69] Ibid., 37.

[70] Department of Corrections and Rehabilitation. Parole And Community Team Resource Handbook.(Sacramento, 2009), 25-39.

[71] Homer U. Ashby, *Our Home Is Over Jordan: a Black Pastoral Theology* (St. Louis, MO: Chalice Press, 2003), 54.

[72] Robert London Smith, *From Strength to Strength: Shaping a Black Practical Theology for the 21st Century* (New York: Peter Lang Publishing, 2007), 125-127.

[73] Karen Lebacqz and Joseph D. Driskill, *Ethics and Spiritual Care: a Guide for Pastors, Chaplains, and Spiritual Directors* (Nashville, TN: Abingdon Press, 2000), 101.

[74] Cheryl J. Sanders, *Empowerment Ethics for a Liberated People: a Path to African American Social Transformation* (Minneapolis: Fortress Press, 1995), 89, Kindle e-book.

[75] A literate witness must sign (if possible, this person should be selected by the participant and should have no connection to the research team). Participants who are illiterate should include their thumb print as well.

[76] Kenneth J. Doka, PhD, MDiv, is Senior Consultant to Hospice Foundation of America and Professor of Gerontology at the College of New Rochelle in New York.

[77] Jim Watkins, The Christian Broadcasting Network, "Dealing with Grief," http://The Christian Broadcasting Network.com/ (accessed July 16, 2011).

[78] 2005-2013 WebMD, LLC, "Depression Overview Slideshow" http://www.webmd.com/depression/slideshow-depression-overview/ (accessed July 26, 2011).

[79] National Center for Biotechnology Information, U.S. National Library of Medicine, "Major Depression" http://www.ncbi.nlm.nih.gov/pubmedhealth/PMH0001941/ (accessed July 8, 2011).

[80] June Hunt, *How to Handle Your Emotions: Anger, Depression, Fear, Grief, Rejection, Self-Worth*, Counseling through the Bible Series (Eugene, OR: Harvest House Publishers, 2008), 80-81, Kindle e-book.

[81] Thomas Hollander, "13 Signs of Anger and How To (Br) Manage Them in Sobriety," *Self Help Magazine*, http://www.selfhelpmagazine.com/article/alchohol-anger/ (accessed August 3, 2011).

[82] Changing Minds.Org, "Fear", http://changingminds.org/explanations/emotions/fear.htm (accessed August 7, 2011).

[83] Merriam Webster, M-W.com, http://www.merriam-webster.com/dictionary/ (accessed Aug 24, 2011).

[84] Copyright © Communicate Now!, Communication-Skills.info, 2003-2009   http://www.communication-skills.info/ (accessed August 4, 2011).

[85] Merriam Webster, M-W.com, http://www.merriam-webster.com/dictionary/ (accessed Aug 24, 2011).

[86] "Good Parenting Skills 101," http://www.wordsyouwant.com/samples/ (accessed August 26, 2011).

Bibliography

2005-2013 WebMD, LLC. "Depression Overview Slideshow." http://www.webmd.com/depression/slideshow-depression-overview/ (accessed July 26, 2011).

2013 Feeding America. "Solid Foundation for Families." Advocating Against Hunger. http://feedingamerica.org/how-we-fight-hunger/advocacy-public-policy/solid-foundation-for-families.aspx (accessed February 1, 2013).

Alcohol and Public Health. Center for Disease Control and Prevention (Washington, DC, 2012) http://www.cdc.gov/alcohol/faqs.htm/ (accessed July 15, 2012).

Alexander, Michelle. *The New Jim Crow: Mass Incarceration in the Age of Colorblindness*. New York: The New Press, 2010, 2012. Kindle e-book.

Andreescu, S. C. *Racial Fairness in Sentencing: A Case Study of Selected Crimes in Jefferson County*. Racial Fairness Commission, Commonwealth of Kentucky Court of Justice. Louisville: Urban Studies Institute, School of Urban and Public Affairs, University of Louisville, 2004.

Ashby, Homer U. *Our Home Is Over Jordan: a Black Pastoral Theology.* St. Louis, MO: Chalice Press, 2003.

Baylor, Barbara T. MPH Minister for Health Care Justice. http://www.ucc.org/justice/health/ (accessed Feb 13, 2013).

Beckford, Robert. *Dread and Pentecostal: a Political Theology for the Black Church in Britain.* Eugene, OR: Wipf & Stock Publishers, 2011.

Boyle, Gregory. *Tattoos on the Heart: The Power of Boundless Compassion.* New York: Free Press, 2011. Kindle e-book.

Bucalos, Dean. "Mission Behind Bars & Beyond." Missionbehindbarsandbeyond.org (accessed February 10, 2011).

Carson, Clayborne. "Martin Luther King, Jr., and the African-American Social Gospel." In *African American Religious Thought: An Anthology*, ed. Cornell West. Louisville: Westminster John Knox Press, 2003.

Changing Minds.Org. "Fear." http://changingminds.org/explanations/emotions/fear.htm (accessed August 7, 2011)

Cleage Jr, Albert B. *Black Christian Nationalism: New Directions for the Black Church.* New York: Luxor Publishers of the Pan-African Orthodox Christian Church, 1987.

Cone, James A. *Black Theology.* Vol. 2. Maryknoll: Orbis Books, 2003.

Cone, James H. "*God and Black Suffering: Calling the Oppressors to Account,*" Anglican Theological Review 90, no. 4 (2008).701-712.

Cone, James H. *God of the Oppressed.* Maryknoll: Orbis Books, 1997.

Copyright © Communicate Now! Communication-Skills.info, 2003-2009. http://www.communication-skills.info/ (accessed August 4, 2011)

Department of Corrections and Rehabilitation. "Parole and Community Team Resource Handbook." Sacramento, 2009.

Donatelli, Elizabeth. "Hundreds of inmates released early across Kentucky." January 3, 2012 . http://www.wave3.com/ (accessed January 3, 2012).

Floyd-Thomas, Stacey et al. *Black Church Studies: An Introduction.* Nashville, TN: Abingdon Press, 2007. Kindle e-book.

Gleissner, John Dewar. *Prison & Slavery - a Surprising Comparison.* Denver: Outskirts Press, 2010. Kindle e-book.

"Good Parenting Skills 101." http://www.wordsyouwant.com/samples/ (accessed August 26, 2011).

Healey, Joseph. "It takes a whole village to raise a child." African Proverb of the Month, November, 1998. http://www.afriprov.org/ (accessed March 1, 2012).

Hengeveld, N., ed. "Micah 6:7-9, CEV." *Bible Gateway.* http://www.biblegateway.com/ (accessed February 11, 2013).

Hollander, Thomas, "13 Signs of Anger and How To (Br) Manage Them in Sobriety." *Self Help Magazine.* http://www.selfhelpmagazine.com/article/alchohol-anger/ (accessed August 3, 2011).

Hopkins, Dwight N., ed. *Black Faith & Public Talk.* Waco: Baylor University Press, 2007.

Horton, Douglas. *The United Church of Christ. Its Origins, Organization, and Role in the World.* New York: Thomas Nelson & Sons, 1962.

Hunt, June. *How to Handle Your Emotions: Anger, Depression, Fear, Grief, Rejection, Self-Worth.* Counseling through the Bible Series. Eugene, OR: Harvest House Publishers, 2008. Kindle e-book.

Johnson, Daniel et al., eds. *Theology and Identity.* New York: Pilgrim Press, 1990.

Johnson, Victoria, CPE Director, Baptist Fellowship Center, Pastoral Counseling Center, Basic Life Skills DMin Project, Louisville, 2010.

Jones, Dionne J. and Stanley F. Battle. *Teenage pregnancy: developing strategies for change in the twenty-first century.* New Brunswick: Transaction, 1999.

Justice and Witness Ministries of the United Church of Christ. *Doing Justice: A Bible study and reflection guide.* Cleveland: United Church Press, 2001.

Kromer, Helen. *Amistad: the Slave Uprising Aboard the Spanish Schooner.* Cleveland, Ohio: Pilgrim Press, 1997.

Law, Violet. "Life after Lockup." NIH: Shelterforce Online. http://www.nhi.org/online/issues/139/afterlockup.html (accessed March 25, 2013).

Lebacqz, Karen and Joseph D. Driskill. *Ethics and Spiritual Care: a Guide for Pastors, Chaplains, and Spiritual Directors.* Nashville, TN: Abingdon Press, 2000.

Lebacqz, Karen. *Six Theories of Justice.* Minneapolis: Augsburg Publishing House, 1986.

Mannoia, Kevin W. and Don Thorsen, eds. *The Holiness Manifesto.* Grand Rapids: Wm. B. Eermans Publishers, 2008.

Martin Luther King Multi Purpose Center. "The Mission." http://www.martinlutherking-mpc.org/home.cfm (accessed March, 2013).

Marshal, Anne. "The Truth about Consequences," *Leo Weekly.* February 22, 2012.

Meadows, Daniel. "What About Digital Storytelling." Educational Uses of Digital Storytelling. http://digitalstorytelling.coe.uh.edu/ (accessed June 9, 2011).

National Center for Biotechnology Information, U.S. National Library of Medicine. "Major Depression." http://www.ncbi.nlm.nih.gov/pubmedhealth/PMH0001941/ (accessed July 8, 2011).

Neuger, Christie Cozad, and James Newton Poling, eds. *The Care of Men.* Nashville: Abingdon Press, 1997.

Noor, Khairul Baharein Mohd. "Case Study: A Strategic Research Methodology." *American Journal of Applied Science* 5 no.11 (2008): 1602-1604.

Pew Center on the States, "Kentucky: A Data-Driven Effort to Protect Public Safety and Control Corrections Spending." (October 2010), http://www.dpa.ky.gov/NR/rdonlyres/1DD65541-F32F-4447-BE51-6D891C20CB6A/0/103_10_PSPPKentucky Brief_print.pdf (accessed February 11, 2011).

Public Health Ontario Partners for Health, The Health Communication Unit. "Summary of Social Sciences." http://www.thcu.ca/ (accessed June 13, 2011).

Ray, Stephen G. *Do No Harm: Social Sin and Christian Responsibility.* Minneapolis: Fortress Press, 2003.

Sanders, Cheryl J. *Empowerment Ethics for a Liberated People: a Path to African American Social Transformation.* Minneapolis: Fortress Press, 1995. Kindle e-book.

Savage, Carl and William Presnell. *Narrative Research in Ministry: a Postmodern Research Approach for Faith Communities.* Louisville: Wayne E. Oates Institute, 2008.

Smith, Donald P. *Empowering Ministry: Ways to Grow in Effectiveness.* Louisville: Westminster John Knox Press, 1996.

Smith, Robert London. *From Strength to Strength: Shaping a Black Practical Theology for the 21st Century.* New York: Peter Lang Publishing, 2007.

Stallings, James O. *Telling the Story: Evangelism in Black Churches.* Valley Forge: Judson Press, 1988.

Thurman, Howard. *Jesus and the Disinherited.* Boston: Beacon Press, 1976. Kindle e-book.

Thurman, Howard. *Deep River: An Interpretation of Negro Spirituals.* Mills College: Eucalyptus Press, 1945.

Townes, Emilie M. *Embracing the Spirit: Womanist Perspectives On Hope, Salvation, and Transformation.* Maryknoll: Orbis Books, 1997.

UCC Mission Statement on Health and Human Services, General Synod 15. http://www.ucc.org/health/pdfs/ucchealthhumanservice-missionstatement.pdf (accessed November 10, 2012).

United Church of Christ Justice & Witness Ministries. *Wider Church Ministries, 2011-2012 Public Policy Briefing Book.* Cleveland: Pilgrim Press, 2011.

United Church of Christ. "Basis of Union," Beliefs. http://www.ucc.org/beliefs/basis-of-union.html (accessed February 2, 2013).

United Church of Christ. "UCC Brand Guidelines" About Us. http://www.ucc.org/about-us/ucc-logo.html (accessed February 11, 2013).

U.S. Census Bureau, Census 2000, Summary File 3 (Kentucky State Data Center, 2000) http://www.census.gov/ (accessed January 3, 2012).

Watkins, Jim, "Dealing with Grief." *The Christian Broadcasting Network.* http://The Christian Broadcasting Network.com/ (accessed July 16, 2011).

Wilmore, G. S. "Black Spiritual Churches." In *African American Religious Studies*, ed. H.A. Baer. Durham and London: Duke University Press, 1989.

Wilson, W. J. *The Truly Disadvantaged: The Inner City, the Underclass, and Public Policy.* Chicago and London: The University of Chicago Press, 1987.

Wimberly, Edward P. *African American Pastoral Care.* Rev. ed. Nashville: Abingdon Press, 2008. Kindle e-book.

Reverend Dr. Jamesetta Ferguson

The Reverend Dr. Jamesetta Ferguson serves as Senior Pastor of St. Peter's United Church of Christ, Louisville. It is there that she focuses on the church's call to spread the Gospel of Jesus Christ to a diversity of men and women who have not yet found the Lord. She was called to Pastorship at St. Peter's UCC in December 2006. This was subsequent to serving as a student in discernment for six months at St. Peter's and 18 months at Plymouth UCC, Louisville. She was ordained and installed as Pastor in July, 2007.

Pastor Ferguson leads in the church's vision to plant and cultivate seeds of necessity in our community through spiritual guidance and community partnerships, continuously seeking opportunities to educate, inform and empower the congregation and community. Under her leadership the Molo Village CDC was established in February 2011. This is a Christian-based Community Development Center designed to promote individual and community empowerment through education, voluntarism and healthy living.

Pastor Ferguson received her Bachelors in Business Administration and Finance from Central State

University in Wilberforce, Ohio in 1976. She graduated from University of Louisville with a degree of Master of Education in 1992. She also graduated from Louisville Presbyterian Seminary with a Master of Divinity degree in December 2006 and a Doctor of Ministry in May 2013.

As a Bi-vocational pastor, Pastor Ferguson is also employed fulltime at the University of Louisville as the Business Administrator and Clinical Practice Manager of the School of Medicine Department of Pathology and Laboratory Medicine and has served in that capacity for over 25 years.

Pastor Ferguson is married to Minister and Deacon Levie Ferguson, and sharing in their joy are their two children: Au'yana Lee and Guante'; a son-in law, Dion Lee; and four grandchildren: Legend, Kennedy, Justice and Masiah.

www.ingramcontent.com/pod-product-compliance
Lightning Source LLC
Chambersburg PA
CBHW060130170426
43198CB00010B/1102